Country Wild

Wild Sierra plums are found growing on rocky slopes in California, Nevada, and Oregon.

David Larkin

with Sabra Elliott Larkin

Country Wild

A David Larkin Book

Houghton Mifflin Company

Boston New York 1998

For information about permission to reproduce selections
from this book, write to Permissions, Houghton Mifflin Company,
215 Park Avenue South, New York, New York 10003.

CIP data is available.
ISBN 0-395-77190-0
Printed in Italy

SFE   10 9 8 7 6 5 4 3 2 1

COUNTRY WILD
is a general introduction to growing things, and is not a field guide.
It is the responsibility of the reader to use authoritative field guides for positive identification
of all of the wild edibles mentioned in this book. The reader should be aware that
any plant substance, whether used in food or medicine, externally or internally,
may cause an allergic reaction in some people. The author and publisher assume no responsibility
for any adverse effect that an individual may encounter in the use of such substances.

Contents

Introduction

Just the place for us, I thought, even though our first look at the house and buildings was in deepest February, with two feet of snow on the ground. But what about the land? What lay on the fields, in the clearings, and among the trees? The conditions made real exploration impossible, but I felt I should try to see something in the fading afternoon light — and remember it. And where was the pond I'd heard of? Up there, I'd been told, in the woods. What about the stream? Again I'd been told there was a bridge over it spanning a steep defile curving around the house. I plowed thigh-high down a slope and could hear the running water under the snow and ice, sounding the pouring of a bottomless cup of coffee . So far, the broker was right; elements of the original description were slowly being revealed.

It was late spring before I could visit the place again and survey it the old-fashioned way, by walking the boundaries. Our attorney fancied a day out of the office, and I think he liked my description of the task ahead — "beating the bounds."

We found one boundary marker, a forked ash tree, and started out. After overnight rain, the sunny but wet and dripping morning was coming to life. We moved along the remains of a stone wall that was slowly crumbling under growing trees of every size and shape, then into a clearing at the end of a seven-acre field we would soon own. "Own" is a bit strong, really. I was not a farmer and certainly not a developer. Borrower or trustee would be a better term, considering how much nature was already there.

I paid attention to the field edges. Nature always moves towards open ground, and this field had not been mown for two or three years. The border between the trees and meadowland is where the greatest variety of plant and insect life occurs. But, according to botanists and biologists, the number of species does not illustrate the fecundity of the area. More likely it's evidence of the precarious nature of existence that prevents any single plant or bug from taking over.

Here I could see grasses such as timothy giving way to cinquefoil, wild strawberries hiding among the hawk-weed, a few dandelions, blueberries in sunny patches. All these are typical late-spring indications of life on the border of a northern hardwood forest. My companion crashed forward while I browsed on the odd strawberry. Now the woods started in earnest, composed of equal amounts of maple, oak, ash, and a few beech and white birches.

I could hear the stream at the bottom of a steep, and what proved to be unstable, ravine. I slid down as gently as possible, remembering from my Boy Scout training that the most valuable and fragile part of any wild environment is the bank of a river or stream. There the most delicate organisms have a tentative foothold and can be destroyed by clumping boots. As the stream cut and rushed its way down this deep little gorge, I noticed how very thin the crust of the soil was. The undermined edges looked like miniature gravel pits. It all looked fresh from the retreating glaciers of 10,000 years ago. The bankside trees had their roots exposed, illustrating the volatility of the stream's action. Inevitably, I dislodged a football-sized stone. A bright orange eft lay in the crater, and as I carefully replaced the stone I was reminded that, to some creatures, this was home.

We had been going for half an hour and I was hearing but not seeing my associate. By the time I caught up with him the morning was beginning to hum. He had removed his shirt as work rate and temperature rose. The Highland Fling, it is said, originated from the human response to the antics of the silent, point-sized black fly. My companion flung and swung away at them, no doubt increasing his body heat and attracting whining swarms of mosquitoes as well. The black flies picked their way easily through my sensible, buttoned-up layers. (That night I had a red-dotted ribbon of bites around my waist.) But this was serious enjoyment. We had gone at the project like a couple of kids.

Even as we walked side-on to the line of the ridge, the ground rose and I guessed we were up to 1500 feet, since more conifers were appearing. After the first springlike rush of flowers on the forest floor, the canopy was closing in and cutting out the light; on the ground were mostly mosses, ferns, and clumps of poisonous hellebore. I did not follow the ridgeline but instead went the way of animal tracks. Animals always find firm going — where the deer walks, man can safely tread.

A month earlier than shown here, the woods had a ground cover of spring flowers that flourished before the canopy of hardwood leaves cut down the light. The white flowers are Dutchman's breeches, which resemble a tiny pair of traditional pantaloons hanging upside down.

A bunch of ramps, picked in early May

I smelled onions but could not see them at first. These were ramps, or wild leeks, identifiable in early summer by their single white globular flower. Only the flower's bud and the lilylike leaves could be seen in the thick, wet rug of greenery. I took note of the location, since it was a big patch to which I would certainly return. Ramps are utterly delicious, with a bold, fresh flavor. Here was my first *new* wild food discovery. And if I'd known about it then, I could have used the crushed leaves, wiped on exposed skin, as an insect deterrent. I did not have to worry about the social implications on that day.

Farther up were what looked like fabulous dens under overhanging rocks, and a rusted traction engine boiler with its funnel hole on one side, crepuscular enough for a large animal's lair. How did it get halfway up a mountain? Perhaps it was pushed down from above before all the second-growth trees came back.

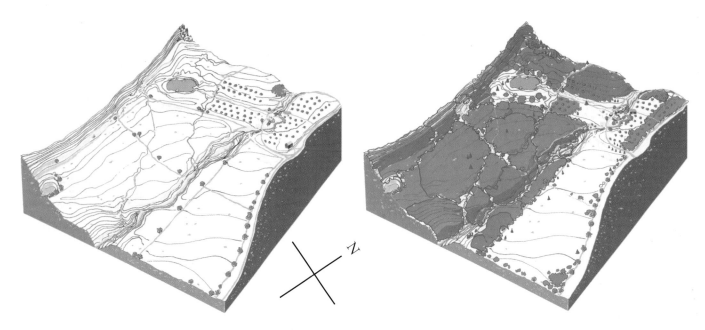

These two sketches show what has happened to our piece of land, typical of the hills of Eastern America that were settled early.
The sketch on the left is based on existing stone walls, surviving apple trees, and standing timber that was not logged. It would have looked like this from the early 1800s until fifty or sixty years ago.
Our property was part of a large family farm that needed more cleared acreage to survive when first established.
On the right is how it looked when we arrived.

After an hour we came to another clearing and a flash of light blue — the pond. Noisy with frogs and beautifully situated on one of the few shelves in the valley, it was big enough to stock with trout. But there was no time to stop now for a pond inspection. Along the the last boundary line, at 1700 feet, I kept finding old apple orchards, old walls, and logging trails that pushed through them both. About all this land had been good for, I thought: sheep, apples, and charcoal.

Back at the car, I was well pleased with what I'd seen by just patrolling the fringe of the property. I really would have loved to have followed the stream as it cut its way diagonally through this piece of country. That would have to wait until I was responsible for it. Nature, in the form of wild plants and trees, was fast reclaiming this once-cultivated area. How did I feel about that? One part of me was annoyed at the silliness of folk trying to farm this shady valley; the other part of me appreciated the evidence of much adaptability and good husbandry. The owners of this land over the past century had known a great deal about the outdoor life, and we were about to follow in their footsteps.

The unmown meadow in early summer

Opposite. A view of the far side of our valley in late summer.
In the distance is Mount Greylock, the highest point in Massachusetts.
The Appalachian Trail runs along the ridge.

A Walk on the Wild Side

When I found the time to explore our piece of land after we moved in, I made for the edges of the fields, the overgrown stone walls, the paths, and old logging trails where the action takes place. There are more varieties of plants, flowers, trees, fungi, insects, birds, and animals to be found here than in the deep woods and wide open fields.

The first summer after our fields stopped being grazed or mowed years ago, here's what happened: By midsummer, the new arrivals, mostly borne by the wind and birds, were annual plants — dandelion, chickweed, and ragweed. The next summer the ragweed poisoned its own patch of ground and itself, dying off after its seeds were blown to another spot. Following came some biennials — Queen-Anne's-lace, mullein, and burdock — stronger plants pollinated by insects. And last, perennials — goldenrod, aster, joe-pye weed, black-eyed Susan, and

maybe the first tiny blackberry and strawberry shoots. This thicker cover, along with insects and seeds, attracted more birds and small rodents, followed by their predators. The first trees moved out from the shady field edges: clusters of spindly white birch, aspen, poplar, and here and there an occasional white pine. These are short-lived for trees, grow quickly and have created cover for the slow-growing oak, ash, beech, and maples that eventually take over. These latter easily outlive humans by a hundred years or so, and die slowly. Underneath, the original pioneer plants would be long gone, but seeds will remain in the ground, waiting for the next cycle of opportunity.

Soon after the land was first cultivated, native plants had to compete with alien invaders. The resident species had numbers in their favor, with generations of dormant

seeds waiting in the ground. But the weeds brought by the colonists were aggressive (a quarter of the plants growing in your meadow originated in Europe). Many alien plants, birds, and animals seem to thrive away from the competition they face in their native lands. Imported starlings, for example, have reduced the population of native woodpeckers, bluebirds, and swallows that have the same nesting patterns. By the same token, on the other side of the Atlantic, the American gray squirrel has almost eliminated the native European red species.

I usually leave a twenty-foot area between the cultivated field and the woods. There, brush cutting and mowing preserve the variety of wildflowers. It's as if this area were regularly grazed and browsed by hoofed animals.

Going back to nature sometimes has its ugly moments, even for those of us who see the unmown field as a potential meadow of wildflowers and butterflies floating in the summer haze. Many of the first invaders have a rough, scrubby look about them that would make them seem at home in an abandoned city lot. Nevertheless, the simple picture above contains many valuable plants. In the foreground are burdock and nettle, sources of food. In the middle ground, goldenrod and aster, valued as medicine. Behind them, in front of a wild apple tree, is the uniquely American Jerusalem artichoke — about the only native in this scene. The tubers from this plant are excellent substitutes for potatoes. A dieter's delight, they are low in starch.

*Lady Bird Johnson is to be thanked for her work in starting the National Wildflower Center
and for keeping alive scenes like this in the Texas hill country. Early settlers stuffed their bedding with
dried flowers of the western coreopsis, shown here, to get rid of fleas and ticks.*

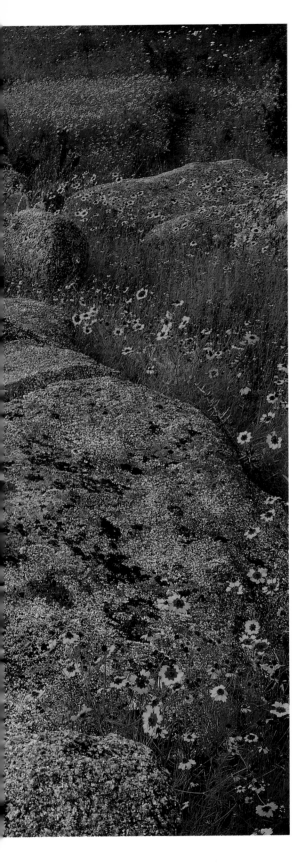

State Flowers of the United States

Unlike the roving birds, which have not been adopted exclusively by each State, the official wildflowers mostly evoke a more varied graphic pattern of stability, even a fragrance, for each area.

Alabama Camellia	Louisiana Magnolia	Ohio Scarlet Carnation
Alaska Forget-me-not	Maine Pine Cone & Tassel	Oklahoma Mistletoe
Arizona Saguaro Cactus	Maryland Black-eyed Susan	Oregon Oregon Grape
Arkansas Apple Blossom	Massachusetts Mayflower	Pennsylvania Mountain Laurel
California Golden Poppy	Michigan Apple Blossom	Rhode Island Red Violet
Colorado Columbine	Minnesota Showy Lady's-slipper	South Carolina Carolina Jessamine
Connecticut Mountain Laurel	Mississippi Magnolia	South Dakota Pasque Flower
Delaware Peach Blossom	Missouri Hawthorn	Tennessee Iris
Florida Orange Blossom	Montana Bitterroot	Texas Bluebonnet
Georgia Cherokee Rose	Nebraska Goldenrod	Utah Sego Lily
Hawaii Yellow Hibiscus	Nevada Sagebrush	Vermont Red Clover
Idaho Syringa	New Hampshire Purple Lilac	Virginia Dogwood
Illinois Native Violet	New Jersey Purple Violet	Washington Western Rhododendron
Indiana Peony	New Mexico Yucca	West Virginia Big Rhododendron
Iowa Wild Rose	New York Rose	Wisconsin Wood Violet
Kansas Native Sunflower	North Carolina Rose	Wyoming Indian Paintbrush
Kentucky Goldenrod	North Dakota Wild Prairie Rose	

Our daily bread, pasta, rice, or oatmeal all come from different forms of grass. It is the greatest single source of nutrition in the world. Grasses are the only plants we cannot do without.

In the Woods

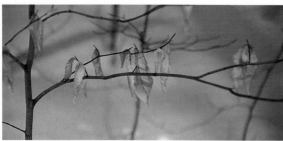

When young, the slow-growing beech protects its vulnerable leaf joints by retaining some of its leaves throughout the winter until new shoots appear; it is sealing its vulnerable abscission zone, where the stem of the leaf joins the branch. The leaves are pushed off by new growth in the spring. As the tree gets older and stronger, it sheds its leaves like other deciduous trees.

Late in the fall is the best time to count the oak trees in your woods. They are the last to lose their leaves.

On previously cleared land, pioneer trees come up fast — first birches, conifers, and aspens, then ash. Size is not important in the first thirty years. After that the disparity becomes apparent. Birches, aspens, and cedars die of old age. They gradually give way to harder woods such as oaks and hickories. Even these will not outlast the slower growing beeches and maples. Left alone, most forests will eventually become almost entirely deciduous.

White pines can be seen behind some sugar maples.

White pine, the most important tree of Colonial America, is easy to work with, and by 1900 it had been almost totally depleted. It was used for shipbuilding (white pine grows straight and long-grained, solid yet supple, making it perfect for masts), houses, farm buildings, furniture, and even matchsticks. Trees were then extensively replanted by hand labor and began to regenerate naturally. White pine appears all over my land and is very quick to grow. For example, tiny saplings were planted along our driveway about twenty years ago by the previous owner. Still young, they are already thirty feet tall and will soon screen us completely from the road. The white pine is easily distinguished from other pines by its cluster of five needles joined together.

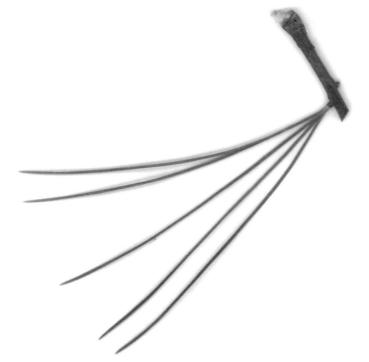

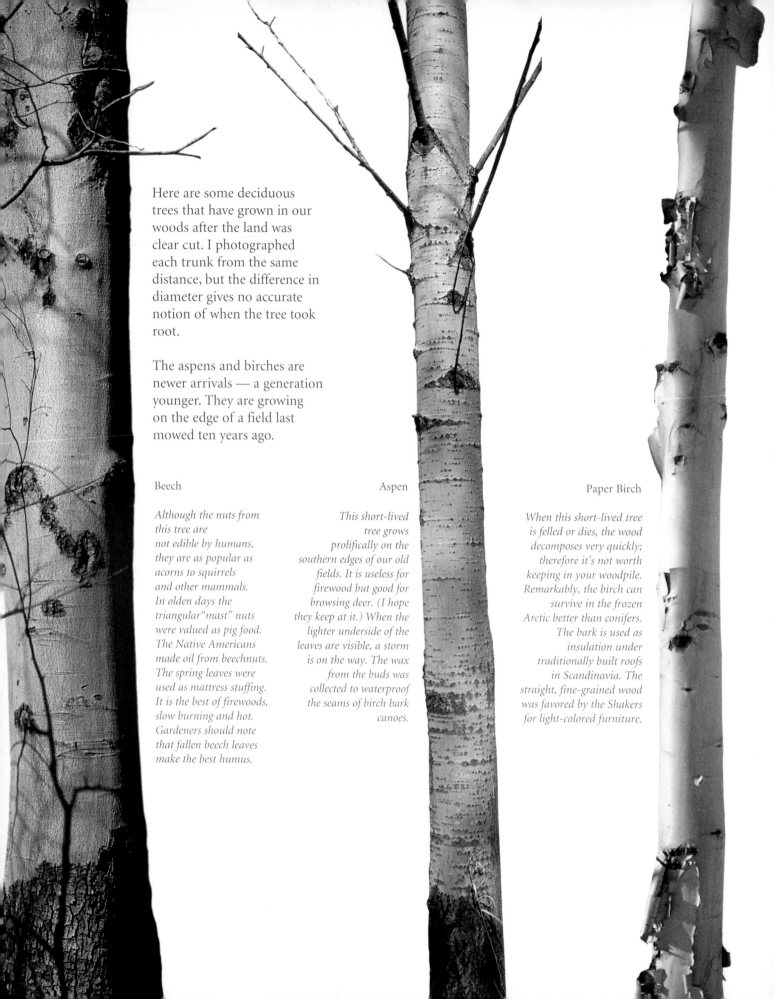

Here are some deciduous trees that have grown in our woods after the land was clear cut. I photographed each trunk from the same distance, but the difference in diameter gives no accurate notion of when the tree took root.

The aspens and birches are newer arrivals — a generation younger. They are growing on the edge of a field last mowed ten years ago.

Beech

Although the nuts from this tree are not edible by humans, they are as popular as acorns to squirrels and other mammals. In olden days the triangular "mast" nuts were valued as pig food. The Native Americans made oil from beechnuts. The spring leaves were used as mattress stuffing. It is the best of firewoods, slow burning and hot. Gardeners should note that fallen beech leaves make the best humus.

Aspen

This short-lived tree grows prolifically on the southern edges of our old fields. It is useless for firewood but good for browsing deer. (I hope they keep at it.) When the lighter underside of the leaves are visible, a storm is on the way. The wax from the buds was collected to waterproof the seams of birch bark canoes.

Paper Birch

When this short-lived tree is felled or dies, the wood decomposes very quickly; therefore it's not worth keeping in your woodpile. Remarkably, the birch can survive in the frozen Arctic better than conifers. The bark is used as insulation under traditionally built roofs in Scandinavia. The straight, fine-grained wood was favored by the Shakers for light-colored furniture.

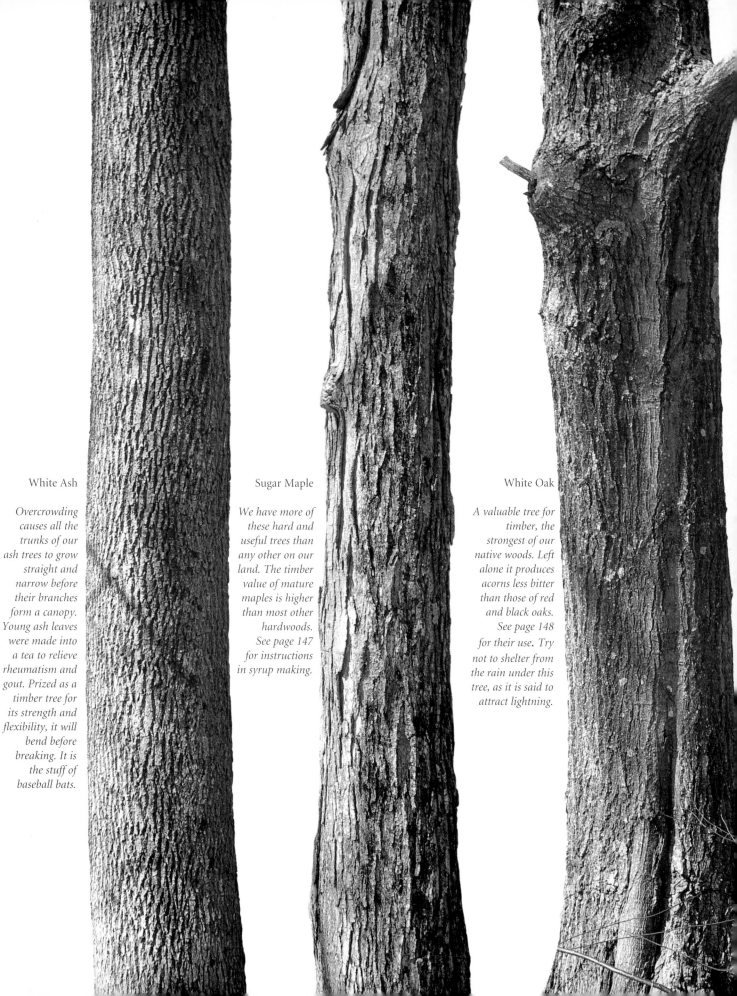

White Ash

Overcrowding causes all the trunks of our ash trees to grow straight and narrow before their branches form a canopy. Young ash leaves were made into a tea to relieve rheumatism and gout. Prized as a timber tree for its strength and flexibility, it will bend before breaking. It is the stuff of baseball bats.

Sugar Maple

We have more of these hard and useful trees than any other on our land. The timber value of mature maples is higher than most other hardwoods. See page 147 for instructions in syrup making.

White Oak

A valuable tree for timber, the strongest of our native woods. Left alone it produces acorns less bitter than those of red and black oaks. See page 148 for their use. Try not to shelter from the rain under this tree, as it is said to attract lightning.

The uniform green of summer leaves gives way to many shades in the fall. This is the best time to identify the trees around you.

Red Maple

Norway Maple

White Oak

Willow Oak

Pin Oak

Shumard's Red Oak

Sweet Gum

Scarlet Oak

London Plane

Yellow Buckeye

Tulip Tree

21

Horse Chestnut
(*Aesculus Hippocastanum*)

This was the first tree I climbed as a kid to get at the shiny nuts we called "conkers." They always looked good enough to eat, but we knew they were poisonous. Our purpose was to play an autumn game of the same name by threading one on a string and taking turns swinging at — and breaking — one's opponent's nut, thus becoming a "conqueror." I think this game went back a long, long time.

As its wood is too soft for timber, the horse chestnut originally was grown as an ornamental. In bloom it is truly spectacular; its white blossoms grow upright like flames on the candles. The tree gets its name from the days when horses with heaves were given the "chestnuts" to keep them from coughing. Supposedly you can keep one in your pocket as a defense against

Sassafras (*Sassafras albidum*)

One of my wife's vivid memories of her days as a young camper is being taken into the woods to collect sassafras and then making tea from it over a campfire. Sassafras tea is generally made from the bark of the roots, or from the whole root, cut into chunks and simmered in water for about twenty minutes or until the liquid turns reddish. The longer it is simmered, the stronger the tea. It used to be quite popular as a "tonic" in late winter and early spring. The principal use of sassafras today is to make the fine powder, from dried leaves, that seasons and thickens soups and stews, particularly in Creole cooking.

Sassafras is a very tall and handsome tree with a fragrant, oily bark, found throughout the eastern half of North America. One of its most interesting features is the display of three leaf shapes, all on the same tree — oval leaves, mitten-shaped leaves, and three-lobed leaves. In the spring, sassafras has small, yellowish-green flowers and bright green leaves, those picked to make powder. In the fall, the leaves turn red.

The early colonists were introduced to sassafras by Native Americans who used it medicinally. The leaves, bark, and roots soon became moneymaking exports to the Old World where, for a short time, sassafras was considered a miracle cure. It was also the flavoring in root beer until recent years when the Food and Drug Administration concluded that the ingredient safrole was a possible carcinogen and banned the use of sassafras oil and bark. This finding is disputed by other experts who feel that the amounts used in the tests were excessive, and that sassafras is safe in the amounts consumed by most humans.

Witch Hazel (*Hamamelis virginiana*)

The native witch hazel is the most mysterious of all trees. Unlike others, it blooms in the late fall after its leaves have turned yellow and dropped. On a walk in the woods you can hear it literally shooting its seeds — up to a distance of thirty feet. The popping sound this makes has led to another common name, snapping hazel nut. If the flowering branches are cut and brought inside, the house will be filled with a pleasant scent. Its forked branches have long been used to divine the spot where underground water can be found. The first settlers documented the use of witch hazel by Native Americans for many medicinal purposes. Extracts and leaf poultices relieved their smoke-irritated eyes, burns, bruises, wounds, and rheumatism, while tea was taken for colds, fevers, sore throats, and dysentery. Today witch hazel extract is sold over the counter for antiseptic or cosmetic use such as cleaning and toning the skin.

Sweet Birch (*Betula lenta*)

Another common name for this tree is the black birch because its bark is dark or blackish. It was, before synthetics, a rich source of oil of wintergreen — try breaking off twigs or scrape off some bark to release the powerful scent. In the early spring, these birch trees can be tapped, just like maples, to capture a sap that can be boiled down for syrup; the sap also can be used fresh from the trees to make the legendary "birch beer."

Birch Beer

5 gallons birch sap
1 gallon honey
1 ounce yeast
1/2 lemon, sliced

1. In a large stainless steel soup pot, bring the sap to a boil. Remove from heat, stir in honey and boil for fifteen minutes.
2. Cool to lukewarm, add yeast and lemon.
3. Cover with a towel and let stand for ten days. Strain and pour into sterilized wine bottles. Let bottles rest in a cool place for two days. Cork tightly, store in a cool, dark spot for two months before drinking.

American Basswood or Linden (*Tilia americana*)

Often called the "bee tree" because its flowers are so appealing to bees, whose honey fom it has an outstanding flavor. This native is a tall tree usually found in moist woods throughout eastern North America. Its yellowish flowers dangle from long, winged stalks in June or July when they can be collected to make a scented tea. Dried flowers are usual, but fresh ones in season also can be steeped in boiling water and strained. Highly prized in Europe, linden tea is soothing to the digestive and nervous systems and is often taken at bedtime to promote peaceful sleep.

Inside the bark

The essence of a tree rises just inside the bark. Under this cover the tree's many sources of energy, vitamins, dyes, fragrances, resins, gums, and tars have been found. Cedars probably saved the lives of the first French settlers in Canada. The Native Americans took a look at the scurvy-ridden crew of the explorer Cartier's ship and concocted for them a drink made from sap that contained a high dosage of vitamin C. Here are a few more uses that have been revealed "under the skin":

Oak and willow bark—still used by bespoke shoemakers for tanning and softening shoe-leather uppers
White hawthorn bark—used in making ink
Shagbark hickory—inner bark used for indigestion
Elder—a salve to treat burns
Hornbeam—tannin
Black walnut—dyes from the nuts
Butternut—brown dye
Eastern hemlock is rich in resin.
Spruce—source of amber, a much-hardened, ancient version of the sticky gum that sometimes works its way out of the trunk. (Incidentally, Howard Hughes' gargantuan airplane, *Spruce Goose,* could only become airborne because its frame was constructed with this light and flexible wood.

Trees are at their easiest to distinguish in silhouette, at the very end of winter when the buds begin to form. Here is a parade of middle-aged and mature deciduous trees. From left to right: Oak, Sycamore, Black Ash, Shagbark Hickory, White Ash, Black Walnut, Mature Ash.

State Trees of the United States

Alabama
Southern (Longleaf) Pine

Alaska
Sitka Spruce

Arizona
Palo Verde

Arkansas
Pine

California
California Redwood

Colorado
Blue Spruce

Connecticut
White Oak

Delaware
American Holly

Florida
Cabbage (Sabal) Palm

Georgia
Live Oak

Hawaii
Kukui

Idaho
Western White pine

Illinois
White Oak

Indiana
Tulip Tree (yellow poplar)

Iowa
Oak

Kansas
Cottonwood

Kentucky
Tulip Tree (yellow poplar)

Louisiana
Bald Cypress

Maine
White Pine

Maryland
White Oak

Massachusetts
American Elm

Michigan
White Pine

Minnesota
Norway (red) Pine

Mississippi
Magnolia

Missouri
Flowering Dogwood

Montana
Ponderosa Pine

Nebraska
Cottonwood

Nevada
Pinon Pine

New Hampshire
White Birch

New Jersey
Red Oak

New Mexico
Pinon (nut) Pine

New York
Sugar Maple

North Carolina
Longleaf Pine

North Dakota
American Elm

Ohio
Buckeye

Oklahoma
Redbud

Oregon
Douglas Fir

Pennsylvania
Hemlock

Rhode Island
Red Maple

South Carolina
Palmetto

South Dakota
Black Hills Spruce

Tennessee
Tulip Tree (yellow poplar)

Texas
Pecan

Utah
Blue Spruce

Vermont
Sugar Maple

Virginia
Dogwood

Washington
Western Hemlock

West Virginia
Sugar Maple

Wisconsin
Sugar Maple

Wyoming
Cottonwood

Watercourses

Fast-moving streams coursing through high woodlands create slippery, moss-covered rocks. This stream dwindled down in high summer to a series of tinkling waterfalls. When tested at this time of year, the water was less acidic than at other times, since it was now pushing through limestone rocks under the granite and gravel. Rushing streams don't leave sufficient sediment in the water for plants — growth is on the banks where they can take root against the current.

The sediment pushed downstream is full of organic material. As the water seeks the quickest way to a lower level, it alters course to form shoals and oxbows of fine silt, perfect for establishing moisture-loving plants. Every small stream bed is part of a larger watercourse that becomes a habitat for many plants. The edges of a track or road following the stream or river, even some distance inland, will be full of variety. The stream is a corridor of life, and also the road for animals and birds. Lower down in the valley, as the stream becomes a river, willows and alders slow and calm the flow; in cultivated areas they often were planted to stay the river's course and stop erosion of its banks.

Even more fertile are the areas connected to an established lake, pond, or slow-moving stream — these are wetlands and marshes, the richest, most valuable and endangered of all natural places. In the past, wetlands, difficult to develop, were therefore rarely settled. More recently, wetlands have been threatened by sophisticated drainage schemes developed by those who see such terrain as cheap real estate or nutrient-rich farmland.

These moss-covered rocks are a breeding ground for black flies.

Marshlands, bogs, and fens change little in appearance year after year, because decomposition is so slow. They have become the best places for recording an area's natural history. Seeds, pollen, timber, and even human bodies with evidence of their last meal still in their stomachs have remained intact for thousands of years in frozen wetlands.

Yellow Pond Lily (*Nuphar variegatum*)

These lilies float gently on freshwater ponds and lakes. They have bright golden, globelike flowers with large, notched leaves that serve as good cover for fish. In late summer the flowers develop pods with large seeds that can be treated like popcorn. Their large rootstocks are best from fall until spring, and can be roasted or boiled like potatoes.

Above is the species known as spatterdock (*Nuphar advena*). If they become too invasive, these lilies can be thinned, and are a good food source. The Native Americans saw them as an important food. In addition to cooking the roots, they roasted the seed kernels to grind into flour.

Tuberous Water Lily (*Nymphaea tuberosa*)

Also found floating on freshwater ponds and lakes, this lily with big leaves and showy flowers provides a generous year-round supply of food. In the spring, the young leaves just unrolling and the unopened flower buds can be boiled and eaten as a vegetable. Next, the seeds can be cooked in oil like those of the yellow lily. Later in the fall, the tubers can be dug and cooked like potatoes.

Water lilies live in an almost self-contained world of their own. Their stems are covered in algae that provide food for newts and water insects and support for frog spawn. The large, flat leaves create pockets of calm water on a windy day. In a pond environment, lilies prefer deeper water than do cattails.

Arrowhead or Wapato (*Sagittaria latifolia*)

This perennial grows on the edges of lakes, ponds, and swamps throughout most of the United States. It has arrow-shaped leaves that vary greatly in size, and three-petaled, white flowers. A favorite food of the Native Americans, Lewis and Clark and other explorers learned about it in their travels. And when the first Chinese were brought to California as laborers, they quickly adopted this plant to supplement their diet.

The small, round tubers attached to the runners of the actual root are the edible part of the plant. They are best collected in the fall, when the leaves of the arrowhead have turned brown. It's a messy and cold harvest, so boots are recommended as well as a small pitchfork or rake to pull the plants out of the mud. The tubers taste rather like potatoes when boiled, roasted, or fried. They are more easily peeled after cooking than when raw.

Marsh Marigold or Cowslip (*Caltha palustris*)

One of the first flowers of spring is the cowslip, which pops up in swamps, wet meadows, and marshy places. It has flowers with five petal-like sepals of golden yellow, and bright green, heart-shaped leaves. In colonial days it was well-known in New England where the leaves, picked young, were a spring tonic, rich in minerals and vitamins provided by nutrients in the drainage from higher areas.

This plant must *always* be cooked, since in the raw state it contains an acrid poison that must be dispelled by the cooking process. It should be boiled in salted water for several minutes, then drained and boiled again for six to eight minutes and drained once more. It can then be tossed with butter and salt. The other edible part is the unopened flower bud first boiled twice to remove the poison, then pickled and enjoyed as a caper substitute.

Purple loosestrife (*Lythrum Salicaria*) grows in ditches, wet fields, and swampy areas. A European import, it is considered a nuisance because of its invasive tendencies and ability to crowd out native species important to birds and other wildlife. However, it does have a lovely spike of purple-pink flowers atop a tall stem. The whole plant, when dried and used as a tea, was a folk remedy for dysentery. The tea also was used as a gargle, and applied as a disinfectant for wounds.

Swamp-cypress (*Taxodium distichum*) spends most of the year with its cone-shaped "knees," which project from submerged roots, poking out of water. Here it is seen in the dry season. The heartwood was harvested for its resistance to decay. Those cypress swamps still remaining are usually protected areas, serving as important, richly organic transitional zones.

Signs of Animals

Animals in the country — unlike well-behaved children — are usually heard but not seen. Tracks in the mud or snow give us the best indication of their actual whereabouts. In addition, their presence is made known by the sounds they make on spring, summer, and autumn nights, the loudest coming from the combat zone on the edge of the forest. (P.D. James, in one of her novels, has a country-wise old tramp say that he has experienced more violence in a hedgerow than in the meanest parts of a great city.) When we see them on our place, the foxes and coyotes are just passing through, more familiar with the details of their large territory than we could ever be. We also see raccoons, skunks, and opossums at dusk, like anyone in the country who owns a compost heap. Our German shepherd and half-wild barn cat have enough sense to let them be. Our dog, as a pup, learned from experience — her encounter with a porcupine required the vet to pull a quiver full of quills from her muzzle.

Animals take flight from a human face and from a body with arms swinging out from the sides; if you want to observe one at close range, walk slowly, take small steps, and hold your arms in — don't look like a scarecrow. Avoid facing the animal directly, so your face doesn't reflect light.

On the following pages are some of our neighbors, their footprints illustrated closer to the eye than commonly seen, and in better light. However adept some animals are at making themselves disappear, they have not yet learned to cover their tracks.

The beaver is busy at night, working as well as eating bark and small twigs. A beaver lodge soon turns into a busy family compound when the four or so kits still in the lodge are joined by the current season's young. A group of ten to twelve all working away together is not unusual, until the lack of raw material forces the newer arrivals to move on. After being close to extermination, the recovering beaver populations are becoming something of a problem in New England and other regions, where free-flowing rivers are blocked and planned reforestation flooded. We see lodges all over our area but rarely see beavers, who are mostly tucked inside until dusk. Beavers can remain underwater for a long time — a beaver can swim for half a mile with one gulp of air.

These **raccoon** tracks, visible in early morning light, were made in wet sand. They will disappear as the sun evaporates the moisture and a breeze begins to blow.

Raccoons occasionally make night raids on our bird feeder, but otherwise seem to have an understanding with our cat and dog. Judging by the way raccoons make off with sweet corn cobs from our compost pile, we are probably wise not to grow corn. Raccoons give country people a lot of pleasure because of their cleverness, but, sadly, we have had to remove two rabid ones from our property. Their common name comes from the Algonquin Indian word *aroughcun* meaning "he scratches with his hands."

Studies of its diet show that the fox does more good for the farmer than harm, consuming more mice, rats, and wild rabbits than it does farmyard ducks and chickens. The red fox was imported from England for the pleasure of fox-hunting landowners. Today's version is a mixture of the red and the native gray fox — which is no fun to chase because it is slow and climbs trees. There are about four million red foxes in the United States, and that number is likely to remain stable because of the competition for food and territory with coyotes, now on the increase. This young fox was photographed just after a pleasurable roll in the morning dew.

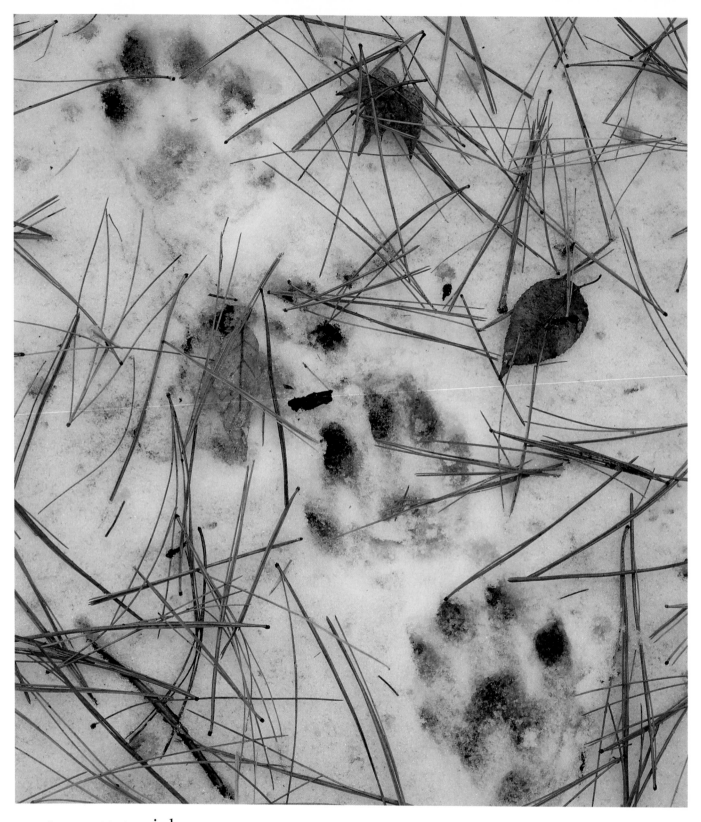

We often see a black **mink** moving at great speed along our stream banks. There may be only one, as they are extremely territorial and their hunting range can stretch for several miles along a river or stream.

The **moose** is the largest member of the deer family. These are the light footprints of an animal that can reach a weight of more than 1,400 pounds. Normally, moose are docile and ignore or shy away from humans. However, don't crowd a bull during breeding season (September-October) or a cow with young ones (May-June) — either one will charge and can cause severe injury.

A fast-running **rabbit** can leave tracks in snow in which the toes do not show, because of the heavy covering of hair on its forepaws. This makes it difficult to ascertain the direction of flight. So consider the relative positions of the rear and front feet of a rabbit in motion. With each leap the closely placed front feet strike the ground first. The rear feet then bypass the front feet, striking the ground ahead of them. Because the rear feet "straddle" the front, the tracks form a triangular shape. The apex of the triangle points away from the direction of flight.

You can find out if a rabbit or woodchuck hole is in use by placing a thin layer of grass or twigs over the entrance.

Black **bears** can accelerate quickly and run at speeds up to thirty mph. They are expert climbers and swimmers but have poor eyesight. All have a sweet tooth and, as we have found out, can do considerable damage to fruit trees and bushes where cultivation borders wild areas. Bears are shy, but, like most animals, bolder when protecting their young. In the unlikely event you are confronted with a bear in the wild, don't face the animal directly, and back away as slowly and quietly as possible. Mother bears will whimper to call their young, and "woof" to warn you away.

During several studies, biologists observed that **deer** are likely to be most active on cloudy and moonless nights when they feel more secure in the open and are least visible to predators. They have excellent night vision and don't need moonlight to see and function well. As human population grows, and deer become more familiar with our behavior, their own habits take some strange turns. Deer are very inquisitive. Plant something, and they come round to see what it is. When they hear the noise of human activity they feel safe. A chugging tractor engine stops, and they look up and bolt. When we are around, silence is what scares them.

Moving out of the cover of woods, this stag is in an overgrown field, a favorite spot for browsing. It is also the territory of the tick that carries Lyme disease. See page 74 on how to protect yourself from this dangerous parasite.

If you ever come across a baby fawn hiding in the long grass, leave it alone; it has not been abandoned. The mother is waiting nearby until you are well away before it comes back.

Except for the mountain-loving hoary marmot, large ground squirrels, comprising **woodchucks** (groundhogs) and prairie dogs, are not popular with those engaged in cultivation. Woodchucks are only interested in young, succulent plants and, as gardeners know, they will travel and expend much effort to reach them. But woodchucks do a lot of good in the wild; their burrows are reused or enlarged by other animals, and in New York state alone, it was estimated that they turned over and aerated 1,600,000 tons of soil in one year.

True hibernation is close to death for some mammals. The groundhog gives us the best example of this phenomenon. After frantic feeding in late summer and early fall, the groundhog retires to a sleeping chamber and walls itself in with dirt. Once asleep, the groundhog's metabolism drops to a very low rate: its body temperature, close to our own at 97F when active, decreases to around 60F; heart rate slows to only one beat per minute; and a breath is taken only once every five minutes. Undisturbed, it will stay in this deathlike sleep for more than five months.

The Great Plains can be brutally hot during the summer, but colonies of prairie dogs use special techniques to keep their burrows cool and comfortable. A typical burrow is a two-ended tunnel between fifty and eighty feet long, with the shape of the entrances key to freshening the underground air.

Prairie dogs build one entrance with dirt piled in a cone-shaped mound around the hole, while the other entrance is low and almost flat. When the wind blows, the difference in elevation creates a vacuum that draws air to the higher entrance from the lower.

The system works so well that scientists estimate even a one mph breeze will create a complete air exchange every ten minutes. Even better, the flat prairie allows the system to work no matter in which direction the wind is blowing.

Gray squirrels are most active just before and during sunrise hours and again late in the afternoon. Smaller and bolder, red squirrels are generally active later in the morning than their gray cousins, but both species may be active during midday hours in the peak of the mast season (when nuts are on the ground). Dull days can contribute to heightened gray squirrel activity. Mornings following clear, moonlit nights may show a decline in squirrel activity, since grays will sometimes feed on bright nights during late summer and early fall. Mornings following dark, overcast nights are apt to be a better bet to find them up and about. A drizzle or light shower probably won't affect activity very much, but windy days reduce movement.

Squirrels are erratic stockpilers of nuts. They hurriedly cart them away, dig a shallow hole, stuff nuts into it, and cover them up. The problem is that they can't always find the nuts again. Scientists estimate that squirrels recover only about half their nuts, despite their excellent sense of smell. This seemingly wasted effort does provide a vital service: the fruits of the oak, hickory, butternut, and walnut trees must be buried to germinate.

The small, bold red squirrel

But squirrels can be a problem. Sometimes the attic of an isolated house is selected as a home, and squirrels are very difficult to move. A friend removed one to find that later it had gnawed its way back in to reach its nesting young. This proved to be an expensive visit, since a carpenter was required for repairs. Eventually the county agent had to come to remove the squatters.

Baby skunks

Our dog has not tangled with a **skunk** so far, but we do have lots of homemade and canned tomato juice ready to help remove the odor if she gets sprayed. Strong soap would be needed to wash our own skin if we were to be victims. One should stay at least fifteen feet away from a skunk's rear end to avoid danger. Skunks are very protective parents and better mousers than cats. They also eat insect pests, digging up lawns in the process, and like to visit the compost heap. On balance, they do more good than harm, but striped skunks are the main carriers of rabies in North America; their territory covers the entire continent.

Porcupines love salt and, oddly, rubber. They have been known to nibble tires that have been on salted roads, wooden tool handles, and leather harness.

The oily meat of the **opossum** is an acquired taste, but is considered by some a delicacy. When threatened or cornered, the " 'possum" exudes a stink, even without a skunk's specialized equipment. Slow moving, it is nevertheless a good cleaner-up of bugs, rotten vegetables, and fruit. One local 'possum makes regular visits to our compost heap and manages to leave a lot of it spread about.

Coyotes have moved slowly back from the West to the East to occupy former wolf territory, picking up some wolf blood on the way and developing into a sub-species, the Eastern coyote. We see them about as frequently as we see black bears, which is not very often. As the territory for each is large, and we can't get very near, we may be looking at the same animals over and over again. Unlike the perpetual-motion fox, coyotes will sit still when caught unaware, but they are just as shy as foxes and will soon move quietly and calmly away. We often hear coyotes at night making their social calls in the next hollow.

This odd-looking trail was made by an **otter** whose heavy tail
pressed into the snow, making a trough. The interruptions were
made by its paws as the otter periodically gave itself a push, rather
like a cross-country skier. Otters can toboggan down slopes
skillfully — often returning just for the pleasure of another ride.
The otter's body is so streamlined it can dive into the water leaving
scarcely a ripple. The otter also can snack on small catches while
swimming along on its back, steering with its tail.

Like Br'er Rabbit, birds, too, are at home in thickets of bramble and thorn.
Small songbirds are attracted to hawthorns and similar species, not only to
keep predators away, but also for the forty-five-degree upward angle at
which the branches and stems grow — perfect foundations for building a nest.

The **wild turkey** was Benjamin Franklin's first choice for the national bird. Perhaps he liked its patriotic red, white, and blue head and neck. Here a couple of young males strut their stuff for females in the flock.

More than 4.2 million wild turkeys have returned to overgrown terrain. The population has rebounded from the end of the last century when it was less than 100,000. The Spaniards are responsible for its name. When seeing it first in Central America, they thought it was related to the Asian peacock, commonly called a *toka*. Another link is the ancient Hebrew word *tukki*.

The bold tracks on the left were made in wet snow. The "arrows" point in the opposite direction to the turkey's progress.

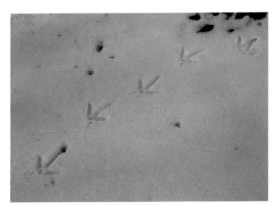

State Birds of the United States

Even in our northern hollow we have permanent residents, and regular visitors that amount to a good third of the species chosen as official State Birds.

Alabama
Yellowhammer

Alaska
Willow Ptarmigan

Arizona
Cactus Wren

Arkansas
Mockingbird

California
Valley Quail

Colorado
Lark Bunting

Connecticut
American Robin

Delaware
Blue Hen Chicken

Florida
Mockingbird

Georgia
Brown Thrasher

Hawaii
Hawaiian Goose

Idaho
Mountain Bluebird

Illinois
Cardinal

Indiana
Cardinal

Iowa
Eastern Goldfinch

Kansas
Western Meadowlark

Kentucky
Cardinal

Louisiana
Eastern Brown Pelican

Maine
Chickadee

Maryland
Baltimore Oriole

Massachusetts
Chickadee

Michigan
Robin

Minnesota
Common Loon

Mississippi
Mockingbird

Missouri
Bluebird

Montana
Western Meadowlark

Nebraska
Western Meadowlark

Nevada
Mountain Bluebird

New Hampshire
Purple Finch

New Jersey
Eastern Goldfinch

New Mexico
Roadrunner

New York
Bluebird

North Carolina
Cardinal

North Dakota
Western Meadowlark

Ohio
Cardinal

Oklahoma
Scissortailed Flycatcher

Oregon
Western Meadowlark

Pennsylvania
Ruffed Grouse

Rhode Island
Rhode Island Red

South Carolina
Carolina Wren

South Dakota
Ring-necked Pheasant

Tennessee
Mockingbird

Texas
Mockingbird

Utah
Sea Gull

Vermont
Hermit Thrush

Virginia
Cardinal

Washington
Willow Goldfinch

West Virginia
Cardinal

Wisconsin
Robin

Wyoming
Meadowlark

Tracks of the eastern coyote

You may or may not ever see the creatures that inhabit the forest, but they are present in higher numbers than you might imagine. For example, based on a survey of 1,000 acres of eastern deciduous forest not far from where I live, an extremely rough estimate of wildlife population follows:

1 billion arthropods (insects, spiders, etc.) large enough to be seen with the naked eye
900 pairs of small nesting birds
25,000 mice
3,500 squirrels
20 white-tailed deer
35 wild turkeys
8 predatory birds (hawks, owls, etc.)
4 foxes
1 bear
1 coyote
plus other assorted animals: woodchucks, raccoons, voles, chipmunks, opossums, skunks, rabbits, etc.

Ranges and Areas

Some animals operate from their dens, or within limited areas; others travel several miles each day in search of food, before returning home. Browsers are always on the move within their own territory.

Opossum—20-30 acres

Black bear—15 miles

Raccoon—2 miles

Skunk—20 acres

Coyote—10 miles

Red fox—2 miles

Gray fox—5 miles

Bobcat, Lynx—25-50 miles

Woodchuck—30-100 acres

Ground squirrel—1 per acre

Chipmunk—2-4 per acre

Gray squirrel—2-10 per acre

Red squirrel—4-8 per acre

Cottontail rabbit—2 per acre

White-tailed deer—1 mile

Moose—2 per square mile

Animal populations have peaks and declines that are quite regular and part of a natural cycle — despite the impact man has on them.

The peak years for rabbits, coyotes, muskrats, caterpillars, and foxes were, and will be, 1981, 1991, and 1999.
Game birds peak approximately every seven years.

Night Eyes

Here are the colors of animals' eyes caught at night by flashlight or headlights.

Deer—bluish white

Wolf, Coyote—greenish/orange

Dog, Fox—pale green/white

Bobcat, Lynx—pale yellow

Raccoon—bright yellow

Opossum—pale orange

Bear—bright orange

Skunk—amber/red

Rabbit—pale violet to white

Jack rabbit—pink

Bullfrog—green

Otter—pale amber

Natural life spans
(*in years*)

Pelican—40-50

Large reptile—25-30

Toad—30

Bear—25-30

Deer—18-25

Domestic cat—17-20

Coyote—12-15

Songbird—10-15

Domestic dog, Wolf—10-15

Beaver—10-12

Otter—10-12

Raccoon—10

Squirrel, Rabbit—10

Fox—8-10

Bat—5

Small rodent—3-5

Shrew—1

The pattern on butterfly wings distracts any predators. To confuse their enemies further, some butterflies taste bad and some edible ones have wing patterns that imitate their unpleasant-tasting kin. I remember that I had to catch white butterflies to save our cabbages (grandfather did not use pesticides), and after picking them off while they folded their wings to lay eggs, I noticed that my fingertips had the highly concentrated stink of rotten cabbage. Defense goes on in the insect world. The light of the firefly would normally be expected to attract predators, but the chemicals that create the insect's glow also make it inedible.

The useful ladybird's bright color advertises that it will taste bad, too.

Above: a blue darner dragonfly
Right: a skimmer

While up at our pond fishing and being still, I become part of the life there. One begins to see how a Thoreau could report on so much activity within his sight. The frogs rarely move, the water boatmen skiff only for short distances, and the dragonflies supply most of the movement and sound from whirring wings as they constantly patrol the pond shore, gobbling up the midges that plague me. The midges and mosquitoes have no hope — it seems that while catching one the dragonfly already marks the next. The dragonfly is able to fly in bursts of thirty mph, flying backward, sideways, upside down, and braking suddenly. I see the value of having cattails, reeds, and sedges at the pond edge; they become carrier decks to launch from when the dragonfly takes off after its prey.

The Canadian tiger swallowtail

Butterflies are more plentiful on sunny days, when flowers release more nectar. The butterflies in our area favor three plants that flower near our house. The yellow Canadian swallowtails come to our chives in great numbers and rarely go anywhere else. Many other species seem to like a very suburban-looking viburnum shrub and, most unlikely, the spotted joe-pye weed (*Eupatorium maculatum*). (It may be truth or it may be legend, but it is said that the common name of this perennial goes back to Colonial times when an Indian named Joe Pye favored it for its healing powers.)

A brushfoot on joe-pye weed

Medicinal plants are often edible, and vice versa. The Native Americans seemed to have had a use for almost everything that grew, and, without always being told, soon found the benefits of the alien plants brought by the Europeans. On preceding pages: Common Wood Sorrel (*Oxalis montana*). The clover-like leaves are a bit sour but make a lovely drink (similar to lemonade) that is good as a diuretic. Steep the leaves in hot water, chill, and sweeten with sugar. Clintonia (*Clintonia borealis*). The young, lance-shaped leaves of this plant taste like cucumber and can be added to salads, but as they grow, the leaves become bitter. It is also known as corn lily. Starflower (*Trientalis borealis*). A wildflower with white flowers on stalks rising above a whorl of green leaves. The Yellow-orange Fly Agaric (*Amanita muscaria* var. *formosa*) mushroom is full of toxic compounds. In the distant past, before the introduction of recreational alcohol, it was eaten to induce hallucination, disorientation, and deep sleep.

Hop (*Humulus lupulus*)

The use of hop dates back to the earliest days of civilization. The Romans ate the young shoots as a vegetable. In Europe it was widely used by the 9th and 10th centuries for beer and ale but not in England until the early 1500s. As recorded by the famous herbalist, John Gerard, hop infusions also were used for skin disorders and as sedatives. Wild hop is a climbing perennial with rough, hairy stems, and leaves that resemble those of the grapevine. It is another escapee from cultivation that grows throughout North America. We find it festooning the branches of our old apple trees. The young tops can be eaten, much like asparagus, in omelets, soups, and other recipes. The parts collected for medicine are the fruits, or strobiles, which are made into tea and given to induce sleep, relieve anxiety and tension, and to aid cramps, coughs, and fevers. At one time dried hop was popular for stuffing pillows, because of its reputation for inducing sleep.

Wild Bergamot or Bee Balm
(*Monarda fistulosa*)

Many people cultivate this perennial because bees and hummingbirds love its nectar-rich flowers clustered at the top of the stem. Native to North America, bee balm can be found in the wild, usually growing in fields or along the sides of sunny roads. Here, in a local field, its pink flowers mix well with black-eyed Susans.

My wife grows a cultivated version with bright red flowers to bring hummingbirds and butterflies nearer the house. The Latin name refers to the Spanish physician, Nicholas Monardes, who discovered its properties in the 16th century. Tea made from fresh or dried leaves relieves colic, gas, and nausea.

Common St. Johnswort
(*Hypericum perforatum*)

In Europe, the flowering top parts of this plant have been dried and used for centuries in the form of an infusion, to relieve depression, anxiety, and tension. St. Johnswort is also highly regarded for the healing properties of an infused red oil, made from its flowers and leaves, reported to have been carried by Crusaders in the Middle Ages to heal their wounds. This oil is also applied for the relief of bruises, arthritic joints, skin rashes, and sprains.

Native to Europe, western Asia and North Africa, St. Johnswort is an import to the United States. It is commonly seen growing on dry banks, in fields, and in clearings. The oblong leaves of this one-to-three-foot-tall perennial have numerous translucent glandular dots that look like tiny punctures when held up to the light. The flowers have five golden-yellow petals and bloom from June to August.

There are ancient superstitions relating to St. Johnswort. Its generic name is derived from the Greek *hypericum* meaning "over an apparition," a reference to the belief that the herb was so unpleasant to evil spirits that one whiff would cause them to disappear. Also, on St. John's Eve, June 24, it has traditionally been gathered and hung in windows or on doors to ward off evil spirits.

St. Johnswort can be cultivated in an herb garden. It likes moist soil and partial shade.

Sweet Goldenrod (*Solidago odora*)

In the 18th century, at the time of the American Revolution, this was one of the major herbs substituted for China tea in defiance of the British "tea tax." Tiny yellow flowers, typical of all the goldenrods, are massed in clusters at the top of the stem. Unlike other goldenrods, however, this one has smooth, toothless leaves three or four inches long that release an anise-like fragrance when crushed.

The leaves, fresh or dried, can be steeped in hot water to make a pleasant drink, often referred to as "patriot tea." It also has been administered medicinally for problems of the digestive system. Sweet goldenrod thrives throughout most of the United States, attracting bees and butterflies when in full bloom. Contrary to popular myth, goldenrod pollen is not responsible for allergic sneezing — the real culprit is ragweed.

Japanese Honeysuckle (*Lonicera japonica*)

In the South, this trailing vine is considered a troublesome weed that moves in quickly to overtake bushes, trees, and empty lots. It was introduced from Asia, where tea made from the flowers is used to treat bacterial dysentery, fevers, and flu. It also can be used externally to relieve sores and swelling.

Adder's-tongue or Trout Lily (*Erythronium americanum*)

When you walk in wet woods in the spring, you often will see groups of these little plants with yellow flowers and mottled leaves. Although you can eat the very young leaves and the bulbs, I don't think I could ever pull up such beauty for food unless I were desperate.

Purple Trillium (*Trillium erectum*)

When you walk through eastern woods in spring and come upon the red trillium, it looks very dramatic with its showy, maroon flower standing in the middle of three broad, oval leaves. Most trilliums should not be picked, but this species is abundant enough that you can pick some of the young, unfolded leaves and add them to a salad. Or cook the leaves in boiling, salted water and serve with butter or vinegar. "Birthroot" is a common name for red trillium. This relates to the medicinal use, by both Native Americans and early doctors, of root tea to induce childbirth, aid labor, and to help stop hemorrhages. The plant also was poulticed for tumors, ulcers, bites, and stings.

Nicker Bean (*Caesalpinia crista*) growing among **Morning Glory** (*Convolvulus arvensis*)

Prickles cover the stems, branches, and leaf undersides of this vinelike shrub, turning it into a formidable hedge. Nicker bean grows along the coast of south Florida, putting out branches up to twenty feet in length, leaves up to eighteen inches long, and fruit pods four inches long. When ripe and dry, the pods split and spill out two round seeds covered with a hard, gray shell. The seeds are sometimes turned into beads for jewelry, and their kernels have been used in folk medicine as a quinine substitute.

Common Yarrow (*Achillea Millefolium*)

We planted yarrow in our garden for the beauty of its small flowers and delicate, feathery leaves, even though it can be found growing wild in fields and all along the roads in summer. We knew this aromatic herb had traditionally been made into a medicinal tea, but it took several years before we got around to making some ourselves. The tops of the flowering stems are collected and dried for this use while the flowers are still in their prime. They should be crumbled and stored in glass jars. To make an infusion, or tea, put dried yarrow and boiling water into a teapot in the following proportions: one tablespoon of yarrow to one cup of water. Let it steep for ten minutes, strain, and then drink. The tea will have a pleasant smell and a slightly bitter taste.

Yarrow tea is reputed to be valuable as a general tonic and as an aid to digestion. Primarily anti-spasmodic and anti-inflammatory, it has been recommended as a medicine for colds and fevers, stomach cramps, gynecological problems, blood circulation, and hemorrhaging of the lungs and kidneys.

Wormwood (*Artemisia absinthium*)

The common name of this bitter, aromatic perennial relates to its use as a vermifuge. It also was thought to be useful as a moth repellent for fabrics, and as a flea deterrent strewn on floors. It has been valued for centuries for its medicinal properties including the relief of indigestion, fevers, rheumatism, gout and liver problems. However, wormwood is dangerous and poisonous when taken in excess. An extract from the root was the basis of the doubly potent addictive liqueur *absinthe* that reportedly killed Toulouse Lautrec and others until the drink was made illegal. Today, with the toxic ingredient removed, it is used as a flavoring for wines, aperitifs and other drinks, and healing teas are made from dried leaves infused in boiling water.

Giant Hogweed
(*Heracleum Mantegazzianum*)

This invasive and noxious plant comes from the Caucasus mountains of Asia, and was privately cultivated as an exotic during the Victorian period in England and the United States. However, it has now escaped such cultivation and invaded the wild in both countries. The plants can grow up to fifteen feet tall. When the stems are broken they produce large amounts of sap that causes severe irritation, swelling, and painful blistering of the skin that requires medical treatment. The hogweed is a relative of the carrot, producing a large, tuberous root that is difficult to dislodge. The sharp-eyed reader may recognize Joanna Lumley, an enthusiastic countryside defender, contending with a decidedly non-fabulous hogweed on her land.

Queen-Anne's-lace, or wild carrot, is a tiny and distant relative of the giant hogweed.

Growing up to six feet tall, **teasel** (*Dipsacus Sylvestris*) has a prickly, thistlelike head with small, purple flowers. It was brought from Europe to grow commercially for the dried heads, which "teased," or raised, the nap on woolen cloth. Today this biennial is naturalized throughout North America and often used in dried flower arrangements.

Skeins of dyed wool from natural colors. They are, left to right: natural, hickory bark and copperas, osage orange and alum, cochineal, tree lichen and alum, log wood and alum, osage orange and copper sulfate, madder root, osage orange and copperas, osage orange and cream of tartar.

Plants have been used in dyes for thousands of years. To prevent the color from fading, a process known as mordanting, or fixing, is necessary to make the color both permanent and richer. Animal or vegetable fibers are usually soaked, boiled, or simmered in the mordanting agent before dyeing takes place. The most common of the agents are aluminum, chrome, copper, tin, and iron in usable form. If this brief introduction captures your interest, there are excellent books available to which you can turn for specific instructions. On this page you'll find examples of colors you can produce from plants, trees, and nuts described in other sections of this book. Of course, there are many other plants good for dye including indigo, famous for its blues.

Natural dyeing of wool from the sheep at Hancock Shaker Village.

Sources of natural dyes

Acorns: bark and acorns give tan

Barberry: roots give yellow and deep green

Sweet Birch: bark offers shades of brown

Blackberry: berries give purple and gray

Bracken: young shoots offer yellowish-green

Chamomile: flowers offer shades of gold

Coltsfoot: leaves give a greenish-yellow

Currants: juice gives shades of lilac to purple

Dandelion: blossoms offer shades of yellow

Daylily: blossoms give yellow, gold, and blue-gray

Elderberry: berries give purple, blue, and blue-gray

Goldenrod: blossoms give shades of lemon yellow to gold

Hickory: hulls and bark give tan

Grapes: ripe grapes give purple

Stinging nettle: whole plant gives greenish-yellow

Beach plum: leaves give yellow

Raspberries: juice gives pink to purple

Sassafras: leaves and bark offer reddish tan, black, and gray

Sumac: berries give yellowish-tan, gray, tan, and brown

Walnut: hulls offer dark brown

The **art** in nature is best appreciated by simple observation while on a quiet walk and, in my opinion, can never be improved upon. But it is there to be used, perhaps best when a natural shape is just borrowed. The graceful and slim paper birch, a favorite of the beavers, was for some Northeast Native Americans the tree of life, which they called *mus'- quch moo'zeese.*

John Hillaby, the great walker and writer of the wild, noticed that "from its bark they made canoes weighing no more than forty or fifty pounds but capable of carrying twenty times that weight; wonderful canoes which, at the first thrust of the paddle, streak across the placid waters of a lake like a bird. Birch furnished them with snowshoe frames and the covering for their lodges. They lit fires with birch; they made horns out of its bark; their papooses were rocked in birchen cradles; they were fed from birchen cups; their squaws were dressed in robes illuminated with the pendulous shapes of that tree, and when they died they were laid to rest among the spirits of the birch forest."

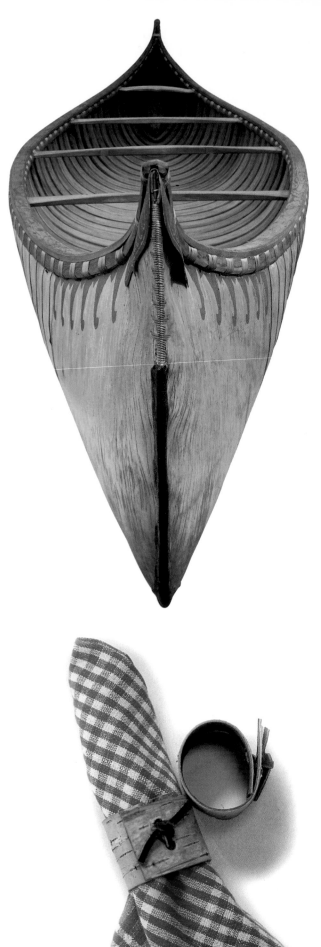

Modestly, all my wife and I have to show of birch bark are some nifty napkin rings, but the carpophore fungus, which grows on tree trunks, does have possibilities, and is fun to work with. While fishing, I scratched out this little picture with the small blade of my penknife and "shaded" it by smudging the surface with a finger. The flattering thing is that, as the fungus dries, the lines become finer.

Walking in the Wild

Over the years, I have made a rough-and-ready **nature trail**. It doesn't have marked spots of interest, but does include a variety of vegetation and changes of terrain and conditions. There is a broad path up to the pond that I mow and keep clear of deadfalls and windfalls. In the spring, it's good for finding fiddleheads, in summer — blackberries, and in winter, it's part of our local cross-country ski trip. Cross-country skis are perfect for touring the woods in winter, and I have seen more wildlife this way than any other, perhaps because the skis move so quietly on the snow.

The pond is a nature trip all by itself. This is the busiest part of our land and, on spring evenings, the noisiest. Teeming is the only word for life there. Each season a new plant or amphibian makes its appearance. This is where we "farm" our rainbow trout for food. I try to keep the fish in balance with the other inhabitants and have learned that if there are more than a hundred in the pond they don't grow much.

Then there is a clearing where I would like to grow blueberries — but it's too far from the house to keep the deer away. The path has evolved from my mushroom route as well as from following game or logging trails. It is not blazed. I don't know anyone today who blazes with an axe: paint is today's tool for orienteering. I would like the time to make more bridges, like this one of hemlock. It fits well in these woods.

Looking after yourself in the wild

The landscape is a place to want to belong to rather than feel lost in. Here are some tips if you take long walks.

Don't drink from a stream below a beaver lodge. A parasite in their fecal matter can cause internal problems.

When in doubt, boil water before drinking. Any stream might have a dead animal in it. Even better, use water-purification tablets.

All streams lead to civilization.

Follow ridges, where vegetation is thinner and you can see farther. However, ridges intersect, so you must keep your bearings by using a compass, the sun, or the stars.

Lyme Disease

Lyme disease was first recognized in 1975, after a mysterious outbreak of arthritis near Lyme, Connecticut. Since then, reports of Lyme disease have increased dramatically. The infection, caused by a corkscrew-shaped bacteria, is spread by the bite of an infected tick. In the northeastern and north-central United States, the deer (or bear) tick is responsible; on the Pacific Coast, the western black-legged tick, and in the southeastern states, possibly the black-legged tick. These ticks are almost impossible to see, no bigger than a pinhead in their nymphal state when they are most likely to feed on a human. They often attach to hidden and hairy areas such as the groin, armpits, and scalp. Adult ticks also can transmit the disease, but since they are larger and easily removed, they are less likely to cause problems.

Lyme disease often is difficult to diagnose because its symptoms mimic those of other diseases. The early stage of Lyme disease is usually marked by chills and fever, headache, muscle and joint pain, swollen lymph nodes, and a circular red rash (in some persons the rash never forms). Late Lyme disease symptoms that may not appear until weeks, months, or even a year after the infected bites include arthritis and nervous system abnormalities.

For greater personal protection outdoors in tick-infested areas, wear light-colored clothing so that ticks can be spotted more easily, tuck pant legs into socks or boots, and shirts into pants, spray an environmentally approved repellent on clothes, and wear a hat.

Once inside, remove clothing and wash and dry it at high temperature; inspect body and scalp carefully. Remove any tick with tweezers as described below. In some areas, ticks (saved in a sealed container) can be submitted to the local health department for identification.

Rocky Mountain Spotted Fever

Rocky Mountain spotted fever is transmitted to humans only by the bite of infected ticks. The American dog tick is mainly responsible for carrying the disease in the East, while the wood tick is the carrier in the West. Most cases occur during late spring and summer when ticks are most active, with symptoms appearing within two weeks of the bite. Most affected individuals develop fever, headaches, bone and muscle pain, and a characteristic rash. Certain antibiotics are usually effective in treating the disease.

Prevention includes wearing protective clothing and tick repellent outside and a thorough check for ticks on clothing and in hair at the end of the day's activities. Dogs and cats that spend time outside should also be combed and checked. These ticks are large enough to be clearly visible.

To remove an attached tick from either a human or an animal, grasp it with tweezers as close as possible to the skin site and pull upward and out with firm pressure. If tweezers are not available, use fingers shielded with rubber gloves or paper, not bare hands. Be careful not to puncture the body of the tick, which may contain infectious fluids. After removal, disinfect the site and wash hands thoroughly.

Outdoors in the cold

The conservation of body heat is key to surviving outdoors in the cold, and if you enter the woods to hike, ski, snowshoe, or camp, be sure to dress properly. As you probably already know, layers of clothing trap air insulating your body, but you will need outer garments made of a synthetic fabric such as GoreTex, which repels strong winds and water and also allows body moisture to escape. If clothes get wet, even from perspiration, insulation is reduced, so it is best to shed layers and put them in your backpack until needed—if you are exercising strenuously or if the day warms up.

Wool or hydrophobic polyesters are generally recommended for layered clothing. Wool, a natural fiber, retains insulating capability even when wet. (Cotton is not good for any layer — it absorbs water.) Polyesters, synthetic fibers, "wick" water away from the skin to the outside of the garment. Wool pants insulate and can be covered with an outer shell. The best-designed pants come with zippers at the bottom that can be opened for ventilation as required. On top, wear a lightweight wool turtleneck under a couple of wool shirts or a Polartec fleece and, depending on the anticipated temperature, a down or synthetic-filled parka under the outer shell.

For the extremities: Wear both hats and gloves with warm linings and outsides that repel water; as socks, once again, wool is excellent — I personally like to put on a pair of silk liners first — but just make sure you don't put on so many layers that you inhibit circulation. For footwear there are many good waterproof and insulated boots available, so, for your own protection, carefully investigate this important item.

Caught in the elements

Stuck in a cold car. A fully charged battery has only forty percent of its capacity at 0°F compared to that at a temperature of 70°F. The colder it is, the weaker a battery gets.

Two inches of ice will support one man on foot. Three inches will support a group in single file. Eight inches will support a small car. One foot, two inches will support a heavy truck. River ice is fifteen percent weaker than pond or lake ice. New ice is stronger than old. In the cold, don't eat without water. Snow eaten in its natural state will cause dehydration. Drink very cold water slowly to avoid digestive spasms.

One can survive without food for twenty days, but without water for only three.

In the snow, the best protection for a night in the woods is a lean-to and bedding of pine boughs. Snow on the roof will keep it warmer. Or, dig down in the snow under a big spruce or pine tree.

You can keep warm by getting the most bedding underneath you. Pine boughs, sagebrush, and rushes work well. In the winter, dry grass can be found at the base of south-facing cliffs. Stones from the campfire well-buried in the earth under your bedding will keep you warm.

In the heat
Light-colored clothing reflects heat. Cover your head. Outer clothes should be loose.

Tannic acid from the bark of hemlocks or oaks can be used to soothe sunburn. For stings, apply wet mud and sumac to soothe and protect.

Just as deer ticks are more likely to be found on the edge of the woods than in them, so is poison ivy. The effect will be worse when one is hot and perspiring.

In the desert, the saguaro cactus holds a lot of water. Water from plants such as the prickly pear is usually pure and has saved lives.

Reindeer moss

Lichens

One wild food not described elsewhere in this book and not very tasty, but a source of emergency rations, is the lichen. These small plants survive through extreme cold and drought and have the remarkable ability to grow in the far North on rocks, trees, logs, and even in sand and gravel. Few species are poisonous to man or animals, and they are rich in carbohydrates. They contain a bitter acid and should be boiled before eating. The most edible species are Reindeer moss and Iceland moss.

Reindeer moss (*Cladonia rangiferina*) This is one of the most abundant plants in northern regions. Look for large, round gray clumps from two to four inches tall, with stems branched like antlers and a woolly surface. Iceland moss (*Cetraria islandica*) can be made into a jelly after boiling. Dark chestnut brown on the upper surface and paler beneath, its forked branches are edged with a row of small spines. It grows in erect tufts.

At the Edge of the Sea

Sea Oats (*Uniola paniculata*)

You will see this graceful brown grass waving in the sand dunes along the southeastern coast. It has most likely been deliberately planted there, after storms or hurricanes, to control erosion. A network of roots, growing just under the surface, helps to keep the sand in place. As these grasses take hold, the dunes begin to provide an environment where bushes and shrubs can become established and further stabilize the area. Sea oats are also grown in inland gardens as an ornamental, and dried for winter arrangements.

Railroad Vine or Beach Morning Glory (*Ipomoea Pes-caprae*)

The railroad vine establishes itself just above the tidal area, often creeping up to a hundred feet in length along sand dunes, helping to stabilize the dunes on the southern coasts. Their glossy green leaves, stationed at regular intervals, are thick and leathery, with two lobes suggesting the imprint of a split hoof, thus giving rise to the species name, *pes-capra*, Latin for "goat's foot." The trumpet-shaped flowers, a beautiful lavender color, open in the early morning and close by noon.

Bayberry (*Myrica*)

Both the Northern Bayberry (*M. pennsylvanica*) and the Southern or Common Wax Myrtle (*M. cerifera*) produce a fruit, called a nutlet, covered with white or gray wax. The wax is boiled from the nutlets and made into aromatic candles or soap which were popular, beginning in Colonial times. The Northern Bayberry is actually a low shrub that grows near the coast from Newfoundland south to Virgina, while the Southern Baybery is an evergreen tree, reaching a height of 10 to 20 feet, growing from New Jersey south to Florida and west to Texas. The leaves can be used as a seasoning in soups and stews but should be removed before serving. And the root bark formerly was used in tea for diarrhea and other internal upsets.

Beach Pea (*Lathyrus japonicus*)

You will find this vine in both East and West coast beach areas and along the Great Lakes. Its pealike flowers, lavender to purple, bloom from June to August. The seed pods look much like ordinary garden peas, only smaller. Pick the young green pods from the vine (do not pull up the plant itself), take out the tiny peas, and cook them for a summer treat. Consult a reliable field guide for more detailed identification, since some members of the *Lathyrus* genus are poisonous.

Rockweed-covered coasts that are pounded by heavy seas are richer with life than those on which the tide ebbs and flows gently. The splashing waves direct more salt onto the shore, enabling the sea life to survive in pools or on rocks.

The use of seaweed as effective fertilizers dates back to the earliest days of agrarian cultures. High potash content is passed on to potatoes, beets, cabbage, and other plants that thrive on large amounts of this substance, which also helps most plants increase their resistance to insects and disease.

The many species of rockweed, small plants growing on rock bottoms between high and low water, are those most commonly collected for fertilizer. Rockweed grows in dense beds. In the spring, old growth falls away and new fronds appear. The old fronds wash onto the shore where they should be raked up and taken off to the compost heap before decay sets in. Alginic acid, the main component of the fronds, is susceptible to bacterial action, the basis of seaweed's energy in a compost heap. Even small quantities can heat up the compost, accelerate its breakdown, and thus its readiness for use.

Three elements meet at the **shore**: water, land, and sky. Not being a sunbather, I prefer to hit the beach in the early morning or evening when the changes of the tide reveal its intertidal, or wrack, zone. In this band are driftwood, polished stones, shells, and the seaweeds. Here, sargassum weed has made its way from many miles out in the tropical Atlantic. On the West Coast, a related species often stows away on oyster shells all the way from the coast of Japan. Sargassum has many uses. Importantly, it contains fatty acids that are highly antibacterial, now being examined as a possible blood anticoagulant. In Hawaii, it is used as a poultice for cuts made by coral. As for food, the western version's leaves can be sun-dried as chips, deep fried in tempura batter, or added to soups.

The shiny, attractive-looking object in the foreground should be avoided. It is a Portuguese man-of-war. Even when dead, it contains powerful poisons that can inflict severe burns.

Found on rocky coasts, mussels have thick shells to withstand the buffeting waves, and a clinging attachment mechanism. They are at their best for eating when the water is cold. Clambering over slippery rocks can be even less pleasant than wading up to to your shoulders in sea water to dig for clams.

Left

A mixture from the Mid-Atlantic. In the center, a blue crab claw rests on the shell of its speckled relative, *Arenaeus cribarius*, common on the coast of North Carolina where this picture was taken. Above it is part of a worm shell (*Vermicularia spirata*). At the bottom is a prized bay scallop shell, smaller than the more common Atlantic deep-sea scallop. Just to the right of the crab shell is an iridescent saw-toothed pen shell (*Atrina serrata*), popular on the Mexican coast where its muscle is eaten, as is that of the scallop.

Right

Cockle and mussel shells like these arrive on southeastern and southern beaches in great profusion. In Florida, where this picture was taken, shells have accumulated over time to form "coqina rocks." The first Colonial building in America, the fort at St. Augustine, was built from this material.

Also seen are the conical and spiraling lightning whelks, often collected as souvenirs. It is said that whenever the opening of a large one is put to your ear you can hear the ocean. Most species of whelk are edible and favored in Europe and the West Indies. They are not popular here because of their toughness. Whelks need much tenderizing and cooking before they attract the American palate. On the top right is a keyhole urchin (*Mellita quinquiesperforata*), a form of sand dollar. At the bottom right is the stiff pen shell (*Atrina rigida*). Its sharp, protruding end is dangerous to the bare feet of waders. (Although you might get lucky — some contain black pearls.)

Wild Food

Edible Plants

It's my belief that the more we learn about the value of wild plants, the more we will want to encourage and protect them. Flower and vegetable gardeners may take special delight in eating the weeds that plague them. Many of the plants displayed on the following pages are held in low esteem by ecologists because they usurp habitats that normally would be occupied by less aggressive native species, and some, although edible and maybe delicious, are too endangered — or too pretty — to consider picking. Some plants, such as daylilies and Jerusalem artichokes, actually benefit by a little thinning. So pick away, but leave enough for animals — or other humans if you are not on your own land.

Each plant is ranked: The higher the grade, the less one need worry about any adverse ecological impact from harvesting it.

A+ Exceedingly common, mostly alien, and often invasive species generally held in low regard by ecologists. Picking these plants is unlikely to make a dent in their ability to perpetuate themselves. Pick as many as you can.

A Common introduced and native species that are plentiful enough to harvest without impact on their availability for future harvests.

A- Common, mostly introduced species, usually found in small patches. Care should be taken to ensure that enough plants are left after harvesting so the plant may continue to exist in that location.

B+ Very common, mostly native species found in good-sized patches where they are often relied upon by native fauna for food. These plants are usually numerous enough to be harvested for as much as one needs.

B Locally abundant native species plus a few aliens that tend to be particular about the type of habitat in which they will grow. Take care to leave plenty so they will continue to thrive.

B- Elusive plants appearing only in a small portion of the habitat that is suitable for them. Occasionally they can be found in large patches, but even then care must be taken to harvest lightly and not endanger their ability to thrive in that location.

C+ Rare enough that careless harvesting could harm them. Only one of every dozen plants should be taken.

C Rare and confined to very specialized habitats, or more common but considered too pretty to pick.

C- Rare native wildflowers or species that should not be picked.

B-	Arrowhead	B+	Jewelweed
A-	Barberry	B+	Kelp
B	Bayberry	A+	Lamb's-quarters
B	Beach Pea	A-	Linden Tree
C+	Beach Plum	A	Mallow
B+	Beech	B+	Maple
B+	Blackberry	C	Marsh Marigold
B	Black Walnut	A+	Milkweed
B+	Blueberry	A+	Mulberry
A+	Bracken Fern	A	Nettle
A+	Burdock	A+	Plantain
B	Butternut	B+	Pokeweed
A	Cattail	B+	Raspberry
C	Chestnut	B+	Sassafras
A+	Chicory	B+	Sea Rocket
B+	Carragheen/Irish Moss	B+	Shagbark Hickory
B+	Clintonia	A+	Sheep Sorrel
A	Clover	A+	Sumac
A	Coltsfoot	C-	Trillium
B	Cranberry	C-	Trout Lily
B	Ground Cherry	A	Watercress
A+	Oxeye Daisy	B+	White Oak
A+	Dandelion	B-	Wild Asparagus
A	Daylily	A+	Wild Carrot
B+	Elderberry	C+	Wild Ginger
B-	Ostrich Fern	C+	Wild Leek
B	Fireweed	B+	Wild Mint
A	Foxtail Grass	B-	Wild Rice
B+	Glasswort	A	Wild Rose
B+	Sweet Goldenrod	B+	Wild Strawberry
B+	Hawthorn	B+	Wintergreen
B	Hazelnut	A+	Wood Sorrel
B+	Jerusalem Artichoke		

Right: a display of drying herbs, seaweeds, and fungi

Enjoy your Weeds

A wise old countryman said, "All plants, when they take their food from the soil, are bound to take the minerals in the soil, and that mineral varies with different plants. Watercress, now, took up a lot of iron, and broom and gorse took up sulphur, so you used the plant itself. Chemists are so clever they get the minerals out of the soil direct, but as we are animals, and plants come between us and the minerals, it does make sense to let the vegetables digest the minerals before we use them."

Feverfew
Tea from this plant, a perennial with small, daisylike flowers, has long been given for colds, fevers, arthritis, and other ailments.

Ramp *or* **Wild Leek**
A choice wild food found in moist, rich woods. It has a white bulb that looks and tastes much like a small leek. It is wonderful either cooked or pickled, and has the same healing and health properties ascribed to onions and garlic.

Pokeweed
Only the young spring shoots (under six inches) are safe to eat; all other parts are poisonous. However, berry teas and root poultices have been used by skilled practitioners in Native American and folk medicine.

Common Plantain
Introduced from Europe, this lawn weed is edible as a salad green or vegetable when the leaves are very young. In folk medicine it is believed to stimulate internal and external healing.

Jewelweed
Both the orange and yellow-flowered jewelweed are annuals whose tender shoots can be eaten before they exceed five inches. The crushed leaves are used for poison ivy rash and other skin problems

Common Cattail
Early young shoots, peeled of their coarse outer rind, cooked and served with butter, are a delicacy often called "Cossack asparagus."

Yarrow
Herbal tea made from the dried leaves is said to be a tonic and a remedy for colds, fevers, and internal disorders.

Wild Chives
Escapees from gardens, wild chives, like their domestic cousins, have lavender flowers and hollow leaves, but are only about six inches tall.

Winter cress
Introduced from Europe, this member of the mustard family is found in wet fields. The young leaves are good in salads or cooked like spinach, and were once used as a poultice on wounds.

Spring-Beauty *or* Fairy Spuds
After the small (one inch) tubers are boiled and the tough jackets peeled, they can be served like potatoes.

93

I was staying with some French friends who lived in the hills above Lyons, when early one morning my host handed me a small kitchen knife "with all the aplomb," as Calvin Trillin once said, "of an English squire loaning a guest his favorite walking stick." He told me we were going to get breakfast. Off we went in the car up into a valley where, in a large meadow, there were already small groups of people on their dew-covered knees.

Our task was to find baby dandelion leaves and remove them as close to the ground as possible. The fine, white leaf stalks, I was told, had the most delicate flavor. Also, as the plant grew, the shaded leaves were less bitter. When we returned, my friend made a wonderful salad from the dandelion leaves, and topped it with croutons and chopped ham. Cheese omelets and fresh bread completed our morning meal.

Common dandelion
(*Taraxacum officinale*)

The dandelion, a perennial, is so admired that entire books have been written celebrating its use in everything from soups and salads to "coffee" and desserts to herbal medicines. This beautiful weed, with its bright yellow flowers, was introduced to North America by European settlers. It is generally believed that its name was derived from the French *dent de lion* (lion's tooth) referring to the toothed edges of the leaves. It is remarkable because every part except the stem can be used as a food or medicine: the young leaves are eaten raw in salads or cooked as a vegetable; the roots can be prepared as any root vegetable or roasted and used as a coffee substitute; the flowers are used to make beer or wine or dipped in batter and fried. In the early days of medicine, even before much was known about vitamins, the leaves (high in vitamins A and C) were eaten as a spring tonic; teas from the roots and leaves were prescribed for all manner of internal problems.

Dandelion wine has a fine, sharp flavor with just a hint of resin, like a mild Retsina.

Dandelion Wine
16 cups dandelion flowers (all green parts removed)
3 pounds granulated sugar
2 oranges
1 lemon
1 tablespoon active dry yeast
4 quarts boiling water

1. Put the flowers in a large, nonreactive pot and add boiling water. Let sit for three days, then strain through cheesecloth.
2. Add sugar, grated orange and lemon rind, and juices to the strained liquid and boil to make a syrup. Cool to lukewarm and add yeast.
4. Let mixture stand for four days in a warm room, covered lightly with plastic wrap.
5. Filter the liquid into a nonreactive container. Cover loosely and let sit until fermentation stops, about three weeks. Funnel into sterilized wine bottles, cork tightly, and store in a cool, dark place for about six months before serving.

Yield: 4 quarts

Ostrich Fern (*Matteuccia Struthiopteris*)
Fiddlehead Fern

Fiddleheads are not a species but an early stage of spring growth when the fronds are young and curled. Several species are edible, but the ostrich fern is considered choice. It is the one you are most likely to see in green-markets and specialty stores. Ferns thrive in rich, wet soil, growing in clumps from rhizomes. Once you have marked their location, be very attentive to their growth, because the emerald-green fiddleheads, covered with dry, brown scales, must be picked when they are no more than six inches high and still tightly coiled. If you miss the moment, they grow increasingly tough and bitter, soon becoming unfit for human consumption, i.e., poisonous. Also, protect your source by picking only half of any clump. Leave the other half to supply energy to the rhizomes for next year's crop.

Other edibles are the cinnamon fern (*Osmunda cinnamomea)*, shaped like the ostrich fern, and bracken (*Pteridium aquilinum*), which has a fiddlehead shaped like an eagle's claw and is covered with silver-gray fuzz that can be rubbed off. Bracken grows in sunny, open places. There have been studies exploring possible cancer-causing substances in bracken, but it is generally believed that bracken fiddleheads eaten in small quantities in spring are not harmful. As with other fiddleheads, they should be picked and eaten only when the fronds are tightly curled.

If you've never eaten fiddleheads, you might wonder why they are so special. I suppose it has a lot to do with the excitement of smelling the earth and picking fresh greens with the grassy taste of spring; they remind me of asparagus and need to be cooked just as carefully. First gently rub off the protective scales with your fingers, or soak the fiddleheads in water until most of the scales float off. Then trim the stems and blanch the ferns in salted, boiling water until tender yet crunchy. They can be tossed with butter and salt or a vinaigrette made with mild vinegar. They can be used as well in numerous recipes of your choice.

Ferns have other uses, too. When I went camping as a kid in the cold English autumn, we stacked bracken around the outside of our tent and stuffed it under our bedding for insulation. Thomas Jefferson, after strolling in the forest of Fontainebleau, wrote, ". . . [I] saw a man cutting fern. I went to him under the pretense of asking the shortest road to the town, and afterwards asked for what use he was cutting fern. He told me that this part of the country furnished a great deal of fruit to Paris. That when packed in straw it acquired an ill taste, but that dry fern preserved it perfectly without communicating any taste at all. I treasured this observation for the preservation of my apples on my return to my own country."

Ramp or Wild Leek (*Allium tricoccum*)

Guidebooks always say wild leeks grow in rich, moist soil in the woods. This is true, but be warned that in a wet spring, or downhill from snowmelt, you will need to wear rubber boots when you harvest them. It also will help to have a garden trowel along to remove the ramps neatly. If you simply pull the plant, the little white bulbs are likely to remain in the ground and you will be left holding a handful of leaves. Wild leeks send up green leaves in the spring that, as they unroll, are flat and lance-shaped, from one to three inches wide and five to nine inches long. Ramps grow in patches, and you probably will smell them before you actually spot the leaves. Later, in June or July, the leaves wither, and a stalk bearing whitish flowers will mark their place.

Ramps are mild tasting, a bit like the garden leek although strong smelling, and are generally considered to be the best wild onion. In fact, they are so highly regarded that spring "ramp festivals," where they are cooked in many ways, are held in West Virginia. Last spring, we tried pickling them in the style of British pub onions and were very pleased with the results. We substituted a milder vinegar for traditional malt vinegar so that the delicately flavored ramps would not be overwhelmed.

Pickled Ramps

4 pounds ramp bulbs
3 tablespoons pickling salt, or other salt without iodine
4 bay leaves
2 teaspoons black peppercorns
2 teaspoons whole allspice
1 teaspoon hot red pepper flakes
2 teaspoons pickling salt
4 cups cider vinegar
2 cups rice-wine vinegar
4-6 pint canning jars and lids, sterilized

1. Wash the ramps thoroughly, remove the green tops and roots, and rinse in clean water. Place in a nonreactive ceramic or stainless-steel bowl, stir in three tablespoons of pickling salt and cover. Let stand overnight.
2. Combine the two teaspoons salt, spices, and vinegars in a nonreactive saucepan. Bring to a boil and simmer for five minutes. Remove from heat, cool and let rest until you are ready to put the ramps into canning jars.
3. Rinse salt from ramps in large bowl of cold water. Drain and repeat three times.
4. Place ramps in a colander and drain. Roll them in paper towels until most of the water has been absorbed.
5. Strain the pickling solution into a large, nonreactive pot and bring to a boil. Add the ramp bulbs, lower to a simmer, and cook for three minutes. Remove from heat.
6. Immediately ladle ramps and liquid into hot, sterilized canning jars. Make sure bulbs are covered by one-half inch of pickling solution. Seal with sterilized lids. Store in a cool place and let them mellow for at least a month before using.

Yield: 4-6 pints

The young bud photographed in early April

Gently does it. The lower part of the stalk can come away if jerked.

The flower in early summer

Common Cattail (*Typha latifolia*)

These tall, spiked perennials grow in swampy or marshy land throughout North America. They spread rapidly. After the plants emerge from the water, they may grow as much as three inches a day, reaching a height ranging from eight to fifteen feet. Once fertilized, the female flower turns into the brown "hot dog," a shape familiar in the country landscape. Cattails are special in that the entire plant is either edible or usable in some way.

In spring, the swollen sprouts can be dug from the mud and eaten raw or cooked. A few weeks later, tender shoots, often called "Cossack asparagus," begin to appear. After the tough outer leaves are removed, the greenish core can be cooked or eaten raw in salads. Soon golden pollen from the flower heads can be shaken into a paper bag and used like flour for pancakes and muffins. Later the roots can be cooked and eaten like potatoes, or dried and made into a high-starch flour.

Cossack Asparagus

24 twelve-inch cattail shoots
2-4 tablespoons butter
Salt and pepper

1. Trim the bottoms and tops of shoots and peel off the coarse outer leaves.
A pale green-white core about ten inches long will remain.
(It will look a bit like a thin leek.)
2. Place in a large, nonreactive frying pan and cover with water.
Bring to a boil, reduce heat to medium, and cook until tender but firm.
Do not overcook or the shoots will become mushy.
3. Drain and dress with butter, salt, and pepper to taste.

The leaves of the cattail can be used for chair seats, the rushes for weaving mats and roofs, and the fluff inside the flower heads to stuff pillows. Native Americans poulticed the pounded root on wounds, sores, and burns; and the root infused in milk has been used to relieve dysentery and diarrhea.

Oxeye Daisy (*Chrysanthemum Leucanthemum*)

This daisy, seen everywhere in summer, has small flowers (about two inches across) featuring a yellow center and white petals. Its leaves, when young and light green, can be added to salads.

Wild Chamomile (*Matricaria Chamomilla*)

Brought to North America by Europeans for their gardens, this annual escaped and is now widely seen in fields and along roadsides. It is apple scented with small, daisylike flowers. The stems grow from six to twenty-four inches tall. The dried flowers are steeped to make a fragrant, pale gold tea traditionally used to relieve insomnia, indigestion, headaches, colds, fever, colic, and arthritis.

Wild Ginger (*Asarum canadense*)

A beautiful plant with twin heart-shaped leaves, wild ginger puts up a small, dark red flower just between its leaves in spring. This is the time to mark the spot in the woods, where it usually grows, so you can come back in the fall to collect the roots when they are at their best. The thin roots grow horizontally just under the surface, thus giving rise to its common name, "snakeroot."

Although not related to tropical ginger, wild ginger has a similar taste and smell, and early settlers dried its root to use as a substitute. You can do the same by washing and slicing the roots and drying them in a dehydrator until crisp. Or, alternately, place them in a 200°F oven for two to three hours. Fresh ginger root is excellent for use in candy, syrups, and drinks.

Wintergreen (*Gaultheria procumbens*)

This low-growing evergreen creeps along the ground in poor or acidic soil, often under conifers in the Northeast. It has the familiar wintergreen fragrance, and its shiny, dark green leaves are attached to the tops of short stems, where white, bell-shaped flowers appear in summer followed by bright red edible berries. Fresh, chopped leaves steeped in boiling water make a refreshing tea that can later be used as a mouthwash. One also can refresh the mouth and soothe irritated gums by chewing the leaves or eating the berries.

Lamb's-quarters (*Chenopodium album*)
Pigweed

Depending on where you live, the locals may call this plant pigweed, wild spinach, or goosefoot — the leaves are shaped somewhat like a goose's webbed foot. The plant is found throughout North America, mainly where the soil has been disturbed — in old gardens or once-plowed fields — and grows from one to six feet tall. The stalks, leaves, and flower heads often turn red in the fall. It was once cultivated as a vegetable in Europe and was actively foraged during World War II when the food shortage was acute. Native Americans also valued the plant for its green leaves and tiny seeds — thousands per plant — which they ground into meal. The seeds are a feast for all sorts of birds ranging from grouse and pheasants to finches, juncos, and sparrows.

Because lamb's-quarters has such a mild taste, many put it at the top of the wild greens list. The young leaves are similar to spinach and can be used, along with the top inch of the young shoots, raw in salads or cooked. The Native Americans ate leaves to treat stomachaches and prevent scurvy, and made poultices for burns.

Stinging Nettle (*Urtica dioica*)

This plant always makes me marvel at human ingenuity. How do you suppose the first person discovered that this stout, four-foot plant with rough, papery leaves and covered with nearly invisible stinging hairs was edible? Or that the pain and irritation it caused to the skin could be eased by jewelweed or dock, often growing in the same vicinity? There's an old country saying, "Where the Lord put a hurt, he also put a cure." Well, you, too, can discover that after nettles are cooked the stingers are deactivated, leaving the greens with a rich, pleasant taste. And they are high in protein and iron as well as vitamins A and C.

Using old gloves and scissors, collect short, tender young shoots (one to two inches) in springtime, or, later in the season, just the tops and young, pale green leaves. They can be braised in butter like spinach or dropped in boiling, salted water, cooked for about five minutes, then dressed with butter and herbs or a vinaigrette. Fresh nettles also can be used to make beer, and dried nettles make a nourishing tea tonic.

Jewelweed (*Impatiens capensis*)

Also called spotted touch-me-not or orange-flowered jewelweed, this is an annual with a juicy stem. It grows from three to five feet tall in wet, shady soil and flowers from June to September. The young shoots, picked before they exceed five inches, can be boiled and eaten as a vegetable. However, jewelweed is probably best known for its medicinal properties. Fresh jewelweed has long been used as a remedy for stinging nettles and poison ivy, as well as cuts, burns, and bites.

Fireweed (*Epilobium angustifolium*)

As you might guess, fireweed grows very well and spreads rapidly on burned lands. It is a tall perennial with showy, rose-to-purple flowers valuable for honey, and lance-shaped leaves. In some areas it is referred to as "wild asparagus" because the young spring shoots can be prepared like asparagus. The young leaves, like spinach, can be eaten as a salad or a cooked vegetable. As with many other plants, the taste grows bitter as the plant matures. The mature leaves can be dried and used to make tea, a folk remedy for dysentery and abdominal cramps. The Native Americans reportedly poulticed the peeled root on burns.

Chicory (*Cichorium intybus*)

During the Civil War when blockades kept many goods from entering Southern ports, chicory root served as a substitute for coffee beans. The fleshy white taproots of the chicory plants are dug up in late summer and roasted slowly until crisp. They are then cut into pieces and ground in a coffee grinder. Many people like chicory's strong taste, and it is an important ingredient today in New Orleans Creole coffee.

Growing from the root is a one-to four-foot stem with small, intense blue flowers. The flowers on individual plants bloom sequentially, but each one lasts only a day. This import from Europe and Asia escaped from gardens and now grows throughout the country in fields and on roadsides. Its young leaves can be used in salads or as a vegetable, but older leaves are bitter.

Chicory flowers are a rough guide to telling the time of day. During its day-long life, each flower closes up at noon for a short period.

Coltsfoot (*Tussilago farfara*)

Coltsfoot is the first wildflower to appear along our dirt road in spring after the ground has thawed. It usually grows on the sides of the drainage ditches closest to the road, where it gets the most light. On a sunny day, the yellow, dandelion-like flowers open and coltsfoot seems to be everywhere, but on a cloudy, rainy day, they close so tightly they are almost invisible. A single flower tops the scaly, reddish stem, which usually has withered by the time the leaves appear. The heart-shaped, jagged leaves were thought to resemble a colt's hoofprint, giving this perennial its common name.

Coltsfoot's generic name comes from the Latin words *tussis ago*, "I drive (out) a cough," relating to the fact that this European import has been used by healers since the earliest times as a remedy for coughs, colds, asthma, bronchitis, and sore throats. The common methods of using coltsfoot include drinking tea from the leaves, smoking the crushed, dried leaves in a pipe, and making the rootstock into candied cough drops. All are believed to be effective in loosening phlegm and relieving a persistent cough. Considered a medicinal herb, coltsfoot has culinary uses as well. Wine or beer can be made from its flowers, and the young leaves can be sauteed or steamed as a vegetable.

In the summer you will see patches of wild day lilies, usually orange or yellow, growing along roadsides all over the country.

Daylily (*Hemerocallis fulva*)

Daylilies escaped from cultivation, but flourished because they were able to adapt easily to a wide variety of soil and climatic conditions. Each flower remains open only for a day, hence the Greek name, *hemerocallis*, meaning "beautiful for a day." The plants keep blooming for weeks in the summer, however, providing an almost constant supply of buds and flowers.

Many foragers consider the buds the most delicious edible part of the plant. Buds should be gathered while small and green and simmered for about ten minutes in salted water. They are then ready to be tossed in butter or a vinaigrette, or sauteed with garlic and summer herbs. The fresh flowers are a delight when dipped in a batter — like zucchini flowers — and fried; and the dried flowers have long been a part of Chinese cuisine. The late fall is a good time to dig up some of your daylily tubers to be replanted elsewhere, or simply to thin out existing plants for better growth the following summer. The small tubers also can be eaten raw or cooked.

Great Burdock (*Arctium lappa*)

Historians believe that burdock was introduced to this country through the tenacious burrs (seed pods) that stuck to immigrants' clothing or to the hide and hair of animals. A biennial plant with extremely large leaves, it grows — sometimes as tall as ten feet — in disturbed ground and overgrown fields throughout the northern half of the country.

The first-year plant is recognizable because it has no flower stalk, but its large taproot is the part most recommended for eating and for medicinal purposes (the second-year root is too tough). The roots grow deep, so it takes a really sharp spade and considerable energy to harvest a good crop. Once collected, wash and peel the roots, leaving the crisp, tasty inner core to be sliced and cooked as a vegetable or even a dessert. In Japan, whole burdock roots are roasted and then served with soy sauce, while in England, burdock beer made from fermented roots is still popular.

Burdock has long been used as a medicine throughout Europe and Asia. Root tea is used for all sorts of internal ailments. It also is applied externally for hives, eczema, and other skin conditions, and leaves have been poulticed on burns, sores, and ulcers.

Japanese Boiled Burdock

Young burdock roots
Soy sauce
Salt

1. Peel and cut young burdock root into pieces the size of wooden matchsticks.
2. Place roots in a nonreactive saucepan, cover with water, add a good splash of soy sauce and a pinch of salt.
3. Bring to a boil, cover and simmer for twenty minutes. Remove lid and simmer until the liquid has almost disappeared and its color has been absorbed by the roots. Watch carefully at the end of the process to prevent burning.

Wild Rice (*Zizania aquatica*)

Wild rice is grown in great quantity in Minnesota, as we all know, but it also can be found in other northern states, in Canada, the Pacific Northwest, and as far south as Florida and Louisiana. Research and early journals show that rice was a staple for the Native Americans who lived where it was plentiful. Also called "Indian rice," wild rice is really an aquatic grass that grows from five to ten feet tall in pure water along the margins of streams, ponds, and lakes with moving water. It flowers in the summer and the seeds ripen at the end of this period, turning a dark slate color. All sorts of birds, ranging from ducks and geese to marsh birds and songbirds, thrive on these grains.

Although we have cooked many pounds of wild rice, we have not had the opportunity to harvest it ourselves. All sources of advice seem to agree, however, that the original Indian method is still the best. When the grains are ripe, a large cloth is spread over the bottom of a canoe or small boat as you paddle among the plants. Then, grasp the stalks and beat the seeds out onto the cloth. The seeds need to be dried and parched in a moderate oven for a few hours and stirred once or twice during the process. The husks can be removed by rubbing the grains between the hands. Store the rice in a clean canning jar. Rinse the quantity you are ready to cook two or three times to get rid of any remaining husks.

Watercress (*Nasturtium officinale*)

You will recognize watercress easily in the wild: the dark green leaves look much like the domestic variety sold in the supermarket. A member of the mustard family, it is a hardy perennial with a peppery bite that does best in gently flowing water. It grows almost everywhere in the United States but likes cool water better than warm, so winter is its best season in the South. After you locate a nearby clump of watercress, investigate your water — even have it tested — to check for pollution and use by cows and other animals. Once you have determined that the water is safe, you can harvest either before the white flowers appear or in the fall, by cutting just under the waterline. Thoroughly wash the watercress and, if you have concerns, eat it cooked instead of raw.

The fresh leaves are high in vitamins A and C and iodine, and traditionally have been used as a tonic and for rheumatism, heart trouble, goiter, and scurvy (one of its common names is scurvy grass).

Watercress Soup

2 tablespoons butter
1 small onion, finely chopped
4 medium potatoes
6 cups chicken stock
Salt and pepper
1/8 teaspoon fresh grated nutmeg
2 bunches of watercress
1/2 cup heavy cream

1. Melt butter in large pot and cook onion until translucent. Add potatoes, stock, and seasonings. Simmer until the potatoes are cooked.
2. Cut watercress leaves from the thick bottom stems. Wash thoroughly.
3. In batches, puree the potatoes, onions and liquid with the watercress in a food processor.
4. Return soup to the pot, adding more stock if too thick, and reheat without boiling. Check seasonings, add cream, and serve.

Serves 4-6, or 10 cups

Ground Cherry (*Physalis species*)

There are many species of the ground cherry, commonly called Japanese or Chinese lantern, husk tomato, or clammy or Virginia ground cherry, that have an edible fruit enclosed in a lanternlike husk. The generic name is derived from the Greek *phusa*, "a bladder," referring to the way the calyx inflates and encloses the fruit after the petals have fallen off. The small berry is ready in late summer or early fall when the husk becomes brown and papery. It can be eaten in jams and pies, or relishes and salsas. Be sure of your identification, since it belongs to the nightshade family and has unpleasant relatives.

Common Milkweed (*Asclepias syriaca*)

As a child, you probably found mature milkweed growing in old fields or along the road, took the pods that were splitting, and delightedly blew the silky seed tassels into the air and all over your friends. The most common milkweed in the Northeast and the one used by wild-food foragers has fragrant pink-purple flowers borne from the central stalk that later develop into long, green pods. Showy and warty, the pods split, revealing tufts of silk hairs that were once widely used in pillows and other bedding. Incidentally, the monarch butterfly also is called the milkweed butterfly because its larvae feed upon milkweed leaves.

The entire milkweed plant has what is known as a "bitter principle" that is mildly toxic to humans and must be removed. The edible parts — new shoots, young leaves, firm little pods, and flower buds — must be placed four times in fresh boiling water for one minute before they can be used in a recipe. This is a lot of bother, so we usually only do it for the pods and flower buds, which have the best taste.

If you want to give milkweed a try, collect the unopened flower buds while they are in tight clusters. After the boiling treatment, the simplest method of preparation is to drop them into boiling water and cook a few minutes before draining and tossing in butter and salt. The pods must be picked while they are small, firm, and not at all elastic when pressed, since at that point they have already moved too far into the seed stage to be edible. After the pods have gone through their four blanchings, they can be used in stir-fries, curries, and the like.

Historically, the milky latex that issues from broken stems has been applied to warts, moles, ringworm, and other skin afflictions. The roots have been used to make a tea to alleviate asthma and rheumatism. Since these uses are potentially toxic, don't try them yourself.

Milkweed and Chicken Curry

20 smallish milkweed pods (boiled as above)
6 tablespoons olive oil
4 large chicken pieces
4 cloves garlic, finely chopped
1 teaspoon salt
1/2 teaspoon ground black pepper
12 cardamom seeds, slightly crushed
1 teaspoon curry powder
1 teaspoon ground cumin
2 tablespoons turmeric
1 large red fresh bell pepper, chopped
2 large onions, chopped
2 cups plain yogurt

1. Boil the pods according to the directions above.
2. Heat oil in a large frying pan, brown the chicken on all sides and remove from pan.
3. Add garlic, salt, pepper, and spices and fry for two minutes over low heat. Add the fresh pepper and onion, and cook until tender.
4. Return chicken to pan and add milkweed pods. Cover and cook over low heat for thirty minutes or more, until the chicken and milkweed pods are tender.
5. Just before serving, spoon two or three tablespoons of yogurt into the pan to thicken the sauce. Serve with rice and a bowl of plain yogurt on the table.

From Wild Food by Roger Phillips (1983)

All wild rose hips have twenty times more vitamin C than oranges. These are Rosa Eglantaria *hips, the Sweetbrier.*

Wrinkled Rose (*Rosa rugosa*)

You are probably familiar with the beauty and scent of wild roses, and you know they grow on thorny shrubs. But you may not have given much thought to their food and medicinal value. This comes from the fruits known as rose hips, or haws, which are very high in vitamin C and have been used for centuries in herbal medicines to reduce infection. Rose hips ripen in the fall and vary in size. They are best picked after the first frost, which softens the texture and sweetens the taste of the fruit. One of the best wild roses for harvesting is the wrinkled, or rugosa, rose, which has an especially large hip. This rose, found along the seashore dunes or roadsides, has five-petaled flowers and dark-green, wrinkled leaves. Sometimes it is actually planted to help hold back dunes or dirt banks. Before cooking, the hips should be cut in half and the seeds in the center scooped out. Since they are high in pectin, rose hips make good jams and jellies.

The oil from rose petals has traditionally been infused into water and applied as a perfume or an astringent. Rose water was also a very popular ingredient in various natural cosmetics when ladies made their own. My wife even remembers her grandmother mixing rose water and glycerin and putting it on her skin to keep it soft.

121

Sea Rocket (*Cakile edentula*)

This peppery plant is a member of the mustard family and, being salt tolerant, is found on the sandy shores of the coastline. From July to September, look for a plant no higher than twelve inches with lavender flowers and succulent leaves roughly three inches long and an inch wide. The leaves and stems can be added raw to salads or cooked in water and eaten as a vegetable. Sea rocket produces two-jointed seed pods that can be eaten or even pickled when small. I can only recommend picking a very small quantity, because sea rocket is important in preventing dune erosion.

The edible prickly pear cactus growing on a Florida beach. See page 132.

Edible seaweeds are full of gelatin, which is the perfect diet food. It has bulk, nutrients, few calories, and is easily digestible. Gelatins from animals have eighty times the calories of those from seaweed.

Slender Glasswort or Samphire
(*Salicornia europaea*)

It is interesting to note that this plant is high in soda; in times past it was collected from coastal marshes or wet alkaline inland spots for use in making soap and glass. Now we search it out as a treat for its delicate, salty flavor. In spring and early summer you will see a bed of emerald green or pink spikes poking up, followed by succulent jointed stems branching from near the base. At this point it looks like "chicken claws," one of its popular common names. Glasswort is usually picked at low tide and is best eaten soon thereafter, although it will keep in the refrigerator for a couple of days. The early spring shoots can be eaten raw in salads, and the larger ones are delicious either cooked or pickled in a mild vinegar. I can remember years ago when samphire was sold in pickle jars or served steamed with crabs. Then fashions changed, and it was forgotten. But now, in more health-conscious times, it has made a comeback and is considered a luxury. One recent summer in East Anglia, a very good village seafood store had a sign in the window saying, "Sorry, Samphire Sold Out."

Cooked Glasswort

1. *Wash the glasswort, leaving the roots intact, and tie in bunches.*
2. *Boil in unsalted water for eight to ten minutes. Remove from the pot, drain, and cut the string.*
3. *Place in a serving dish and dress with melted butter and pepper.*
4. *Each stem contains a woody stalk. Pick the glasswort up by the root and bite the stem, gently pulling the fleshy part from the woody center.*

Giant Kelp or Bullwhip Kelp
(*Nerocystis wetkeana*)

There are many edible varieties of kelp, but the giant kelp, found in the ocean from Alaska to California, is the most dramatic. The stem, or "whip," can grow to more than one hundred feet in length and is attached to an air bladder with long, thin, trailing blades. This kelp usually grows on rocky bottoms and is harvested in summer or early fall. It is best to use the ones rooted to the bottom

for food, but just after a storm there is often fresh kelp readily available on the beach. The hollow stems are washed, peeled, cut into pieces, eaten like cucumbers, or pickled.

Native Americans of southeastern Alaska used the long stems as fishing line. Powdered kelp is carried in health food stores for its nourishing properties, since it is especially rich in calcium, phosphorous, and potassium.

Carragheen or Irish Moss
(Chondrus crispus)

Irish moss is found along the Atlantic Coast from North Carolina northward and on the coasts of Europe. Attached to submerged rocks by small disks and growing in dense beds, the reddish-purple fronds are gathered at low tide. Often you can harvest Irish moss cast up on the shore. Tough and elastic when wet, and brittle when dry, the fronds release a form of gelatin called carrageenan. It has been used for centuries as a thickener in cooking soups, stews, and puddings, especially blancmange, in which the fronds are cooked with milk and then sweetened. This seaweed has been traditionally served in foods for the sick because it is easy to digest and nutritious: it is high in iodine, vitamins A and B, protein, and minerals. After collecting, wash and dry your Irish moss and store in clean, dry canning jars. You will need roughly half a cup of the dried, crumbled carragheen to thicken four cups of liquid.

Basic Soup

1 cup dried carragheen
5 cups chicken stock or water
3 slices prosciutto, finely chopped
3 cups carrots, diced
3 stalks celery, diced
1 teaspoon fresh thyme, minced
Salt and pepper

1. Soak dried carragheen in stock or water for fifteen minutes, remove with slotted spoon, and chop into small pieces. Strain stock or water to remove any sand or grit.
2. In a soup pot, bring the stock to a boil, add the carragheen, prosciutto, carrots, celery, and thyme. Cover and simmer for forty-five minutes.
3. Puree the mixture in a food processor or blender.
4. This base can be enriched to taste by adding sauteed mushrooms, diced cooked chicken, chives, etc.

Serves 4-6, or 8 cups

Mesquite (*Prosopis glandulosa*)

The Native Americans of the Southwest, where the mesquite thrives because of its massive root system, have made good use of this small tree over the centuries. On its spreading branches, appearing on rounded spikes, are small, green flowers, delightfully sugary to suck, followed by tender pods that can be cooked and served as a vegetable. Dried and ground, the seeds make meal that can be used in breads and puddings or stored for winter use. Mesquite seeds also have served as animal feed; the bark has been turned into skirts, twine, and baskets.

Pinyon Pine (*Pinus edulis*)

The soft, small nuts of all the Pinus species growing in the western United States and Mexico are edible but vary in quality. Pine nuts are high in protein and fatty oil (3202 calories to the pound!). The seeds were removed from the cones in quantities by Native Americans, who stored them for the winter. They also raided the nests of pack rats to get at their stashes. Nuts from *Pinus edulis* are generally considered to be the tastiest, especially when roasted. Ground into flour, pine nuts can be added for body and flavor to everything from pancakes and cakes to soups and stews.

Edward Abbey said in *Desert Solitaire*, ". . . Pine nuts are delicious, sweeter than hazelnuts but difficult to eat; you have to crack the shells in your teeth and then, because they are smaller than peanut kernels, you have to separate the meat from the shell with your tongue. If one had to spend a winter . . . with nothing to eat but pinyon nuts, it is an interesting question whether or not you could eat them fast enough to keep from starving to death."

There have been stories of "foodies" in Europe falling out of trees similar to pinyon pine during desperate attempts to get at *pignolis* for their fresh pesto.

The remarkable pinyon was used in many ways by the Native Americans — for its resin to waterproof baskets and relieve rheumatism, sore throats, and boils; for its needles to make tea; and for its inner bark and young wood eaten as trail food.

Yucca (*Yucca filamentosa*)

Yucca is usually thought of as a Southwestern desert plant, but several of the thirty-odd species are hardy in the North. Nearly all of them have stiff, swordlike silver-green leaves growing in clumps at ground level. A tall, leafless stalk rises up in late spring bearing a spike of fragrant, waxy flowers. The creamy white flower petals are a treat in salads and are sometimes candied. After the flowers drop off, seed pods appear that should be picked while green, with their tender, white seeds still inside. The pods can be simmered in water for about ten minutes, drained, tossed with salt and butter, and served as a vegetable. Yucca root was used medicinally by Native Americans in poultices or salves for skin sores and diseases. *Yucca glauca*, better known as Soapweed, is a species whose roots contain saponin, used to produce an excellent substitute for soap.

Prickly Pear (*Opuntia species*)

Many edible species of *Opuntia* grow in the United States in dry soils, including the seashores of both coasts; but the desert variety has the largest and most delicious fruit. These perennials have flat, spiny pads and bear showy yellow flowers between May and August. The pads are protected by waxy, almost impermeable hides that conserve water, allowing them to grow in arid regions. The flowers develop into thorny knobs, or fruits, that turn red as they ripen in the late summer and early fall. Also known as Indian figs, the fruit pulp is good raw or made into juices, candy, and preserves. The young pads of the prickly pear can be collected in the spring, peeled, sliced, and cooked like green beans.

Prickly Pear Jam

24 ripe prickly pears, peeled and
coarsely chopped
2 cups sugar
1 cup water
2 tablespoons lemon juice
2 tablespoons orange juice
1 package pectin
4 pint canning jars, sterilized

1. Place chopped pears, sugar, water, lemon and orange juices in a heavy nonreactive pan and bring to a boil. Lower heat and simmer, uncovered, stirring occasionally for about forty minutes, or until the mixture has thickened.
2. Add pectin if you like an extra-firm jam.
3. Ladle into sterilized jars and seal with sterilized lids.

Yield: 4 pints

Opposite: Prickly pear preserve being made.

Mushrooms

In the summer, I can rarely go for a walk without turning it into a foray, and from the first week of July onward I'm after mushrooms. After ten years I know where the spots are, so all I wish for is at least one day a week with a good rainfall. We are lucky to have a field bordered on its north side with mature oak trees stretching for about a quarter of a mile. Under the circle of their branches, on mossy, grassy ground, yellow chanterelles grow, smelling like apricots. They obviously like the diffused shade. They do not pop up like the bigger-capped mushrooms but are closer to the ground, sometimes hiding under thick grass and leaves. When you find one, you will spot others nearby, and when you get down nearer to their level, your eye begins to sharpen and you'll find more and more. Chanterelles, like most other ground fungi, grow in a ring, and you'll soon recognize which way the ring is curving.

Sometimes I find large clumps of black chanterelles, which prefer a little more gloom and a layer of dead leaves to push through. They never, in my experience, reappear in the same place, and they are hard to see, but finding one means finding them all. They seem to escape the attention of slugs, too. At the same time, among the less-edible boletes, I have found choice ceps. Getting them before the slugs do means an early start.

I'm unsure of the mushroom cycle, so I always leave some unpicked. When I remember them, I spread dry cow manure in places that have been good to me.

Before we get to particular species and ways to serve them, here are some words of caution. Most mushrooms are not dangerous, even if not worth tasting, but some are *extremely dangerous* to eat. I have been over-cautious, and although often proved wrong, I'll probably remain that way. To avoid ever getting mixed up with the pure-looking, white and deadly *Amanita* family — including the Death Cap — I avoid all mushrooms that are white with white gills underneath.

Years ago, I found an enormous ring of very large brown-capped mushrooms that ranged in size from that of buns to small loaves. They smelled and looked good, so I sliced through one. Its stalk and gills began to turn green, then azure. I checked through my guides, made a spore print, and was convinced that it was not poisonous. But that color change did me in — it just didn't seem right, so I threw the mushrooms away. After checking the deposit from the spores the following season, I found out that what I did not have the nerve for turned out to be delicious yellow-cracked boletes.

Last year in early fall, I went on a fungi walk conducted at a nearby environmental preserve. It was to be led by a mycologist who was, I found, replaced by an amateur. The morning did little to add to my knowledge of fungi. Before embarking on the stroll, our leader gathered us around his well-thumbed guidebook and told us never to look at mushrooms printed in color because the printing is never accurate. One sensible thing he did say was that making a spore print was the safest way to understand a mushroom. During the walk he admitted that a mushroom's color meant little to him because he was colorblind. I left about then, certain that the colors of a spore print would confuse him further. Here is what sensible gatherers and mycologists say:

Never eat any mushroom unless you can absolutely identify it as edible.

Buy several good reference guides such as *The Audubon Society Field Guide to North American Mushrooms* or Roger Phillips' *Mushrooms of North America* (which is well-printed in color with accurate scale markings) and use at least two for positive identification. If you have any doubts, take sample mushrooms to an expert in your area.

Be warned. Looking like a pile of freshly baked brioches, this tasty-looking clump is made up of poisonous Jack O'Lanterns.
They were growing out of the base of a dead tree on a bank of our pond. When I went back to the spot at night, they were glowing a pale green.
Imagine these in your stomach!

Yellow Chanterelle *(Cantharellus cibarius)*

The summer we moved to the country, I immediately began walking about our fields and woods searching for mushrooms. At first I found none, but within a few days there was a heavy downpour that I hoped would cause some to appear. So I put on my boots and, with high expectations, went out to our long, mown field bordered with oaks and conifers. And there they were under the oaks — bright yellow chanterelles, smelling slightly of apricots, looking like spilled egg yolks. I picked one or two and ran back to the house to show them to my wife. She insisted that I prove they were not the poisonous Jack O'Lanterns, which I did with the help of my best field guides. Chanterelles are found in July and August in the Northeast, from September to November and later in the Northwest. If you have located a spot where some might grow, go out early in the morning after a rain and pick them before the slugs get busy. Since these mushrooms push up through the ground, they usually need to be rinsed under cold running water to remove dirt. Large, older ones should be sliced down the middle to remove any little invaders.

Our yellow chanterelles keep appearing every year in the same places. One very rainy summer we had such an enormous quantity that even after giving them to our friends and preparing all sorts of recipes, we had enough left to dry and freeze. We found that complicated recipes tend to obscure the delicate taste of chanterelles, so we stick with the following simple one. We serve it, with a dry white wine, for lunch accompanied by a green salad or as a first course at dinner. My favorite moment in the enjoyment of this recipe is when the flavor of the chanterelles and herbs combine in the juices soaked into the toasted French bread.

Chanterelles with Herbs

8 1/4 inch slices French bread
2 tablespoons olive oil
2 tablespoons unsalted butter
6 cups fresh chanterelles, cleaned,
pulled apart lengthwise in 2-4 pieces,
depending on size
1/4 cup chives, chopped
1/2 cup mixed fresh herbs, chopped (sum
mer savory, tarragon, thyme, oregano)
1/2 cup fresh parsley, chopped
1 teaspoon salt, or to taste
Freshly ground black pepper

1. Toast bread and place two slices on each of four warmed plates.
2. In a twelve-inch skillet, heat butter and oil until bubbling. Add mushrooms and cook over medium-high heat, tossing frequently for about four minutes, or until soft. The mushrooms will release a good amount of juice.
3. Add the chives, herbs, parsley, and salt and toss to blend for about one minute.
4. Spoon the mushroom mixture with its juices over the toast. Top with freshly ground pepper and serve immediately.

Yield: 4 servings

My best spots for finding chanterelles and ceps are under the low branches on the north side of mature oak trees. I go over the area lightly with a scythe — just enough to keep down the brush.

You have to get down low when there is thick grass. The chanterelles are hard to see at first, but you'll soon develop a sense of where they are likely to be, and you can also pick up their scent — it's just like apricots.

A camper's feast. Here the chanterelles are sauteed with cured ham, a precooked potato, and a handful of parsley.

Giant Puffball
(*Calvatia gigantea*)

It is absolutely amazing to happen upon a puffball — especially a large one. They seem so perfect and white sitting there on a lawn, or in a meadow or old pasture. Common from summer to late fall, they are usually between eight and fifteen inches across, though there have been reports of huge puffballs weighing many pounds. Puffballs are choice edibles only while the flesh is snow white and firm; they become bitter as they age and a tinge of yellow appears. Slice small puffballs from top to bottom to make sure there is no outline of a stem or gills, which would mean you accidentally picked up a poisonous *Amanita*. There are many ways to cook puffballs: for a low-fat version, try slices brushed lightly with olive oil and baked; or for an Oriental style, dip slices in tempura batter, deep fry, and serve with sauce.

Sauteed Puffballs

2 tablespoons canola oil
2 tablespoons butter
1 small puffball, sliced
1/2 cup flour
1 egg, beaten
1/2 teaspoon salt
1 cup fresh bread crumbs
1/4 cup grated parmesan cheese

1. Heat oil and butter in skillet until bubbling.
2. Dust mushroom slices with flour and shake off excess.
3. Dip into beaten egg and salt, then press both sides gently into mixture of bread crumbs and parmesan.
4. Add enough slices to cover bottom of skillet without crowding, cook quickly until golden brown, and drain on paper towels. Repeat until all slices are cooked. Serve hot.

Serves 2

Yellow Morel (*Morchella esculenta*)

Mushroom foragers are almost always secretive about places where they find their prizes — especially about where they find morels, which have a very short season, seldom more than a month. Morels require a near-perfect combination of temperature and moisture to produce abundantly. They occur from March to June, growing either singly or in groups in burned-over spots, old apple orchards, and under ashes, oaks, beeches, and maples. I have the best luck when the apple trees are just losing their blossoms. Morels are distinguished by their cream to brownish yellow, conical and honeycombed cap, and by the fact that both the cap and stalk are hollow. There is also an edible black morel (*Morchella elata*). You must carefully check the morels you find to be certain they are true morels: "false" morels are similar in appearance to the edible but contain toxins that render them dangerous.

If you find a quantity of morels, refrigerate them or start drying them immediately. Otherwise, rot will set in quickly. Morels need to be prepared before cooking to make sure no little creatures are in the cavities. Slice them in half from top to bottom, trim the stems, and rinse under cold running water. Drop them into boiling water for two minutes to blanch, then dry them on paper towels.

Dry morels by cutting them in half, trimming the base of the stem, and rinsing under cold running water. Afterwards, dry on paper towels, thread on strings, and hang them up to dry in a warm spot. Store in sterilized canning jars with clean tops. When ready to use, blanch for two minutes in boiling, salted water.

Morels in Cream

6-8 large, fresh morels
1 tablespoon unsalted butter
1/2 teaspoon chopped garlic
1/2 cup heavy cream
1 tablespoon chopped parsley
1/2 teaspoon salt and pepper, or to taste

1. Prepare fresh morels as directed above. Cut into large pieces, saute in butter for three to four minutes.
2. Add garlic and cook for two minutes.
3. Add cream, parsley, salt, and pepper and simmer for five to ten minutes.

Good with grilled polenta or pasta.

Serves 2-4

Cep or King Bolete
(*Boletus edulis*)

This mushroom, prized for its flavor and texture, is large with a reddish-brown cap that sometimes grows up to ten inches around and a stem that thickens toward the base. The generic name, *Boletus,* comes from the Greek word *bolus,* meaning lump. You can look for ceps on the ground under conifers and deciduous trees from June to October. Edible young ceps have white pores under the cap; as they age, the pores turn yellow and must be peeled away from the cap and discarded. Although excellent fresh, boletes may be preserved for the winter by washing them carefully, slicing, and placing them in the sun or in a food dryer. When reconstituting dried mushrooms, carefully remove the mushroom pieces, then strain the liquid to remove any sediment or grit. You will be able to find many recipes using both fresh and dried ceps, but the following is excellent for revealing the taste without a lot of fuss. You also can create a marinade using different herbs, soy sauce, etc., to suit the character of your meal.

Grilled Ceps

Oil for grill
2 large ceps
4 tablespoons olive oil
2 tablespoons balsamic vinegar
1/2 teaspoon salt

1. Prepare a gas or charcoal grill. When ready to cook, oil the grill.
2. Clean mushrooms and remove stems.
Leave the caps whole and slice the stems in half lengthwise. Place in a shallow dish.
3. Whisk together oil, vinegar, and salt and pour over caps and stems. Marinate for twenty minutes, turning several times.
4. Remove from marinade and grill for approximately four minutes on each side.

Serves 4

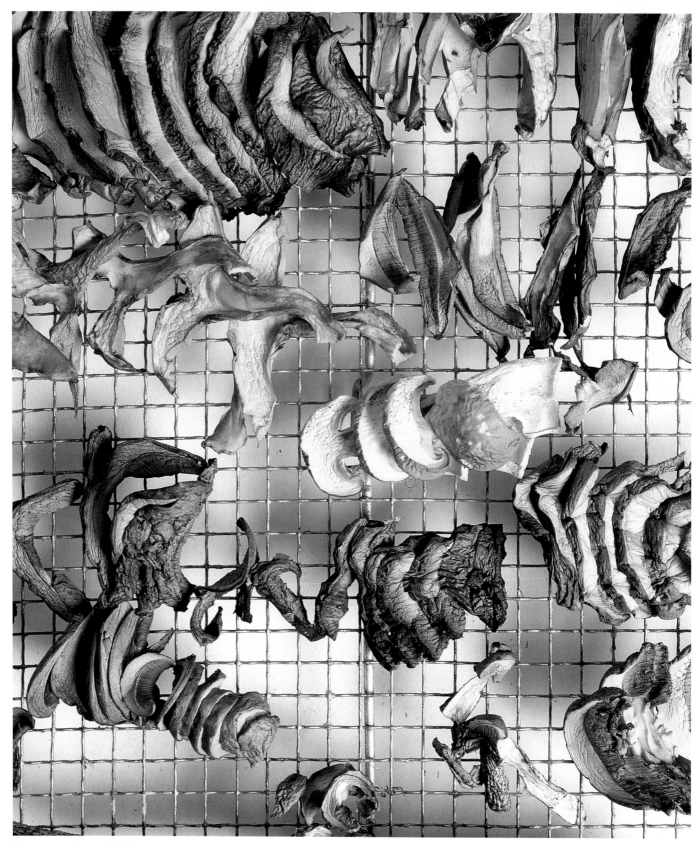

Drying a good crop of sliced ceps

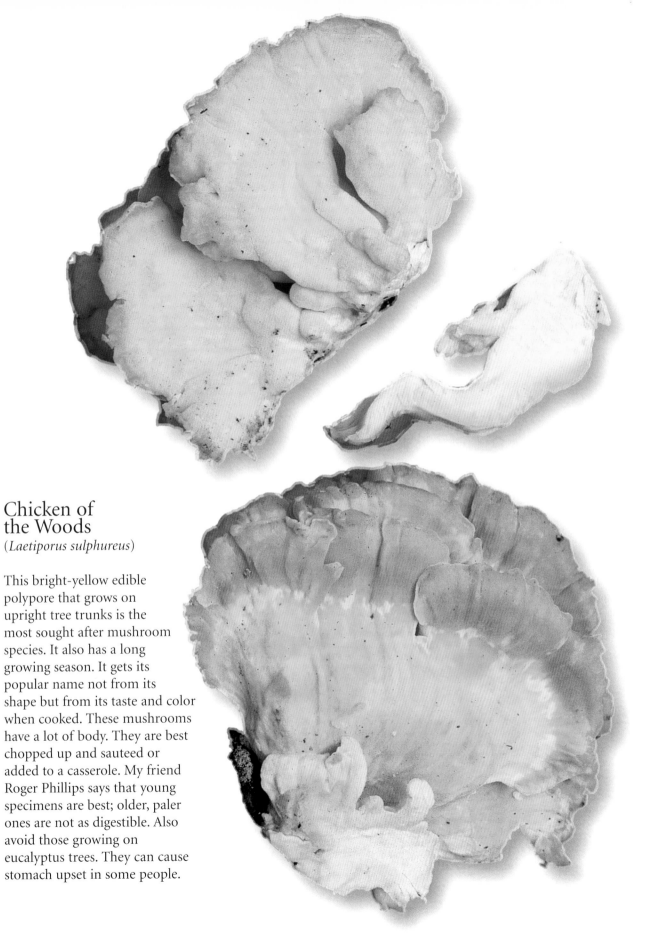

Chicken of the Woods
(*Laetiporus sulphureus*)

This bright-yellow edible polypore that grows on upright tree trunks is the most sought after mushroom species. It also has a long growing season. It gets its popular name not from its shape but from its taste and color when cooked. These mushrooms have a lot of body. They are best chopped up and sauteed or added to a casserole. My friend Roger Phillips says that young specimens are best; older, paler ones are not as digestible. Also avoid those growing on eucalyptus trees. They can cause stomach upset in some people.

Black Trumpet (*Craterellus fallax*)

We rarely find black chanterelles in our area because of the temperature and rainfall. However, every year we patrol our property, searching under beeches, oaks, and other deciduous trees. When we find them, they are in a big clump several square yards across. Dark gray to black, and small — 3/8 to 3 1/4 inches wide — these trumpet-shaped mushrooms are well camouflaged by the color of the earth and by fallen leaves so that one must look quite carefully. Found throughout North America from June to November, black trumpets have a delightfully woodsy taste and smell, both fresh and dried. The first time I reconstituted these dried mushrooms,I was delighted to find they still had a strong odor and flavor.

Gnocchi with Black Trumpets

1 1/2 pounds mixed fresh mushrooms: black trumpets,
 meadow mushrooms, and ceps
1 tablespoon unsalted butter
2 cloves garlic, peeled and minced
1 cup unsalted chicken stock
1/2 cup cream
2 tablespoons chopped chives
Salt and freshly ground pepper
1 pound gnocchi

1. Clean black trumpets and trim ends; remove stems from meadow mushrooms or ceps and reserve for another use. Cut caps into 1/4-inch slices.
2. Melt butter in large skillet. Add garlic and saute four minutes over low heat. Add mushrooms and cook until they release their liquid. Add chicken stock and simmer for five minutes. Stir in cream and simmer for another five minutes. Add salt and pepper to taste.
3. Boil the gnocchi until tender but firm, and drain. Toss with the mushrooms and garnish with chives.

Serves 4 as a first course.

Meadow or Common Field Mushroom
(*Agaricus campestris*)

These mushrooms start popping up on lawns and mown meadows in our part of the country in late August and sometimes last as late as October. In warmer parts of the country they can continue on into winter. When out driving, we keep a bag in the car just in case we spot some along our route. (Visiting friends often think we have gone crazy when we stop suddenly for no apparent reason and dash out of the car.) The cap of this mushroom is smooth and whitish and the gills begin as pink, later turning chocolate to blackish brown. Another similar-looking choice edible is the horse mushroom (*Agaricus arvensis*), which is larger, bruises yellow, and smells of anise when young.

Note: Because the deadly white *Amanitas* grow in similar habitats, you must be positive about your identification. The photograph above is particularly useful. Although we picked these at the same time, you can see the difference in gill color between the smaller, younger ones and the larger, mature ones. The *Amanita phalloides*, or Death Cap, looks just like these from above, but its gills are white.

The field mushroom is a relative of the cultivated white button mushroom but with a stronger, nuttier taste, so that you can substitute it in your favorite recipes.
In a good wet year, there may be so many mushrooms that you will want to save some for the winter. From our experience, we feel freezing is better than drying. Frozen mushrooms can be used in many ways. Following is our method:

Mushroom Preparation for Freezing

3 to 4 pounds field mushrooms

1. Cut off the soil-covered ends of stems. Clean mushrooms as thoroughly as possible, but do not soak in water.
2. Chop mushroom caps and stems very coarsely, and place in a metal colander.
3. Pour about an inch of water in the bottom of a large pot. In the center of the pot place a stainless-steel bowl wide enough to catch drippings from the bottom of the colander.
4. Rest the colander on top of the pot and cover with aluminum foil.
5. Bring the water to a boil and steam for ten minutes, stirring after five minutes.
6. Remove colander with mushrooms from pot and set aside. Strain juices from the bowl to get rid of any grit.
7. Add mushrooms to strained juices, place in containers, and freeze.

Yield: 4-6 cups

Maple syrup can be extracted from several species of maple tree. In the North and East and as far west as the prairies it's the sugar, black, or rock maple; silver, or white, maple; and the box elder. Farther on it is the bigtooth maple in the high canyon lands of the West and Southwest. The Oregon maple has some syrup, and the plains Indians also used the box elder.

Native Americans first taught the French how to tap maple trees. The French then improved the methods by using European utensils of brass or copper to boil down the sap. Before the end of the 17th century the Indians were using kettles. But they, like some syrup makers of today, did not like the continuous refining to obtain a pale, sweet syrup, arguing that the darker syrup tasted better, with the flavor of the forest.

"In late February, 'Sap Moon' in the Algonquian calendar, Indian men and women set up camp in the sugar bush. In central Illinois, sugar maple thrives on the rough and somewhat steep slopes that descend to the waterways, and may dominate the forest. These thick stands of hard maple are self-seeded.

But a productive sugar grove requires human care and attention. Indians removed brush that impeded movement from tree to tree, girdled and burned out old trees, and tended replacement saplings. By piling snow around the base of producing maples, collectors could delay the bursting of the leaf buds and extend the sap season by a week or more."

From *The Maple Sugar Book*, Helen Nearing and Scott Nearing.

"In established groves, Indian women tapped trees by making horizontal gashes in the trunks three or four feet above the ground and inserting cedar 'spiles' at a downward angle, allowing the sap to drip into elm or birch bark buckets. Before the importation of kettles, they collected the sap in wooden troughs, boiled it by dropping hot stones into the sap and stirred until granulation occurred. The sugar they stored in 'mococks', sewn birch bark bags. Men cut wood, made fires for heating the stones or kettles, and hunted and fished for camp. The integration of men's and women's work, the place of sugar-making in the seasonal round marking the end of winter, and the delightful, sweet product all lent a festive air to the occasion. Children loved to pour the boiling sap on the snow to cool into chewy candy."

From *Food Products of the North American Indians*, Commissioner of Agriculture Report, 1970.

It is easy to make your own syrup if maples grow on slopes down to your house. The old way was to drill a hole and then make a spout from a hollow sumac twig, and let the sap drip into buckets. Downhill, the buckets are emptied into a large tank or cauldron. But the long outdoor hours, depth of snow, and hidden roots may make the early season's enthusiasm fade. Now, with plastic tubing, some simple plumbinglike joints, and gravity, the sap can make its way down to you on its own.

The warmer days, increase of light, and cold nights make the sap rise. The trees need to be at least twelve inches in diameter and healthy (tapping does no harm to the tree). You can put more than one tap in bigger trees. The bigger the crown of the tree (i.e., more leaves), the more sap. Whether in a sugarhouse or outdoors, the fire under the tank needs to be constant and the liquid, mostly water, must remain at the boiling point, 212F. As the water evaporates, the boiling point slowly rises. When the temperature reaches 7F above the boiling point of water, the syrup is usually considered done. A neighbor who makes syrup told me the other day that the skill involved in the process is to avoid burning the syrup as the water evaporates. If the sap is not strained and clear as it flows into the boiling receptacle, the sandy sediment at the bottom will burn just like an unstirred pot on a hot stove. Also, he said that towards the end of the season, although the sap may run well, it becomes "milky," losing some sweetness. (I tasted it from the pipe: it was sweet to me but not to him. He detected more acid, plantlike characteristics in the liquid.)

Here's what it can all boil down to:

One small tree can yield up to twenty gallons of sap throughout the season, enough for one-half gallon of syrup.

A sugarbush of more than a hundred trees, ranging from small to large, in a lower than average year, can still produce more than sixty gallons of syrup.

It's best, but not necessary, to tap on the south side of a tree.

Never drill deeper than three inches into the tree.

The hole should tilt slightly downward toward the outside of the tree, about ten degrees.

Insert one tap for every foot of diameter.

Always keep the liquid covered.

Sap was rarely boiled down in the home kitchen, as the vapor is sticky.

Hot syrup is dangerous, like molten lava.

You need 1/4 of a cord of hardwood to boil down 100 gallons of sap.

Assorted nuts. From left to right: English walnuts, butternuts, bitternut hickory nuts. Below: Black walnuts, shagbark hickory nuts, shellbark hickory nuts.

Acorns (*Quercus species*)

There are dozens of species of oak found throughout North America, divided roughly into two groups: the white oaks, whose nuts have smooth shells and sweet kernels; and the red oaks, whose nuts have woolly shells and bitter kernels. Acorns were an important food supply for Native Americans and later for the explorers and colonists. They also provide sustenance to all sorts of wildlife ranging from quail and turkeys to bears.

All acorns are good to eat, but the bitter ones have a higher tannin content. Tannin, however, is soluble in water, so shelled whole or roughly ground acorns can be soaked in water to leach it out. Today most people soak the nuts in boiling water, repeating the process with fresh water until the liquid turns clear. The nuts, high in fat and protein, are then dried, roasted, and ground finely for breads, pancakes, and puddings.

White oak acorns

Black Walnut (*Juglans nigra*)

This strong and beautiful tree, native to North America, has fast been disappearing because it is so highly prized for furniture and also very slow growing. In our field, we have planted some that we hope will be cherished by the next generation. The nuts, round with a smooth husk, ripen in September and October and fall to the ground. Wear gloves when you pick them up because the husks have a brownish dye that will take a long time to wear off your skin. If you spread the walnuts out in the sun until they are partially dried, it will be much easier to take off the husks. The shells are incredibly tough, so it takes a firm whack with a hammer to crack them, and a pick to get out all the meat. Black walnuts have a very rich flavor that gives a distinctive taste to cakes, pies, cookies, and sauces.

Native Americans used tea made from the inner bark as a laxative, and juice from the nut husks to treat ringworm and inflammation.

Above: Pecans, mockernut hickory nuts.

Butternut (*Jugleans cinerea*)

Confederate soldiers often were called "Butternuts" because their homespun clothes were dyed with the green nut husks and the inner bark of this tree.
In earlier days, Colonial settlers and those on the frontiers made the same use of the butternut harvest.

The butternut can grow as tall as eighty feet, bearing oval nuts 2 to 2 1/2 inches long, with sticky husks.
In addition to eating the nutmeats, Native Americans boiled the nuts to release the oil that was then skimmed off and used like butter. Oil from the nuts also was used to cure tapeworm and fungal infection. Like the black walnut, the inner bark was made into a tea used as a laxative.

Hickory (*Carya species*)

These North American trees are somewhat similar to walnuts, but have smaller fruits with husks marked by four ridges when mature. The hickories with the best edible fruit are pecan (*C. illinoensis*), shagbark hickory (*C. ovata*), big shellbark hickory (*C. laciniosa*) and mockernut hickory (*C. tomentosa*). The time to gather the nuts is in the fall as soon as they have fallen to the ground. This group of nuts was eaten by the Native Americans in great quantities, as well as by birds and animals such as raccoons, bears, and even rabbits.
In the spring, sap from these trees can be collected and boiled down to make syrup.

Black walnuts

Hazelnuts

Barberry jelly and catsup being served with a haunch of venison

Common Barberry (*Berberis vulgaris*)

Most of us probably have not had the opportunity to eat anything prepared from the tart, red fruit of the barberry. However, judging from old cookbooks like Miss Leslie's successful *Directions for Cookery*, first published in 1829, it was a 19th-century favorite for jellies, conserves, and catsups. The thorny shrub grows as tall as ten feet, and bears clusters of berries in August and September. It can be found in old fields and thickets from southern Canada as far south as Missouri and Delaware.

Barberry Juice

Cook one pound of ripe barberries in one quart of water until soft. Cool. Crush berries and drain through cheesecloth. Sweeten to taste with honey or sugar.

Miss Leslie's Barberry Jelly

Take ripe barberries, and having stripped them from the stalks, mash them, and boil them in their juice for a quarter of an hour. Then squeeze them through a bag; allow to each pint of juice a pound of sugar; and having melted the sugar in the juice, boil them together twenty or twenty-five minutes, skimming carefully. Put it up in tumblers with tissue paper.

Common Strawberry (*Fragaria virginiana*)

The common strawberry is much like the cultivated strawberry but on a smaller scale, and is one of the widest ranging of our wild fruits, thriving everywhere except in arid areas. Early explorers recorded them as being most abundant in sunny meadows and fields. Ripe from June to August depending on the elevation and latitude, wild strawberries are small and grow in clusters close to the ground. It takes a long time to accumulate even a cup, but the intense flavor is well worth the effort.
(I noticed when in Sweden that folk out for a walk in the short summer, when finding these *fraises des bois*, had a clever way to carry them home. The strawberries were threaded on a stalk of timothy.) It is best to enjoy them fresh and plain, perhaps rolling them in a bit of confectioner's sugar or adding a little cream. However, if you have time to pick a large quantity, use them in any recipe in place of cultivated strawberries.

Common Blackberry
(Rubus alleghaeniensis)

Blackberries grow in old fields, hedgerows, and the sunny edges of woods in just about every region of the United States. Their arching stems feature beautiful white flowers in spring, followed by juicy black fruits in late summer. When picking I always wear denim jeans and a long-sleeved shirt to avoid being scratched by the thorny canes. My wife's grandmother said ladies used to protect their hands by wearing worn cotton or old leather dress gloves when picking blackberries and raspberries. Blackberries can be eaten plain with sugar and cream or cooked in many ways. My favorite, deep dish apple and blackberry pie, announced the end of summer in my childhood, because both fruits ripened at the same time and were freely available. The pectin in the apples held the filling together. In addition, the tender tips of the new canes that appear in spring can be peeled and sliced into salads; and the dried leaves can be used to make tea, my personal favorite substitute for the real thing. We especially like to make blackberry brandy, because when you uncork the bottle out comes the scent, as well as the taste, of summer.

Blackberry Liqueur

Pick very ripe berries and, if they have been growing in a protected, unpolluted spot, you can choose not to wash them. If you do wash them, dry in one layer on paper towels. Fill a quart canning jar with the berries, and pour in a good quality cognac or Armangnac until it reaches the top. Cover tightly with the lid and place in a dark, cool spot for three to four weeks. At the end of that time the berries will be pale, since their color and essence have leached into the cognac. Strain through a sieve, pour the liquid to the top of a glass bottle with a tight cork or other cap, and let it rest for at least a month in a cool, dark spot. The liqueur is at its best for about eight months.

Raspberries (*Rubus* species)

We have a thicket of raspberries in a clearing near our kitchen windows. When the berries are ripe and the sun beats down on them, the fragrance wafts all the way into the house. This is our signal to get out and pick quickly before birds, bears, and other animals come to partake of the feast. When the raspberries are ripe and warmed by the sun, their taste is perfect. A great many go straight into the mouths of the pickers rather than into their baskets. These wild red raspberries (*Rubus strigosus*) have almost six-foot-long reddish canes covered with many fine thorns. They spring up in disturbed soil, clearings, the edges of woods, and roads where seeds have been deposited by birds. Depending on the specifics of climate, the fruit can be picked from June to October.

In good years there has been such an abundance that my wife has made everything from vinegar and jams to tarts and liqueurs. We tend to prefer recipes in which the raspberry flavor is predominant. Two of them follow:

Raspberry Sorbet

8 cups red raspberries
4 tablespoons framboise liqueur
1 1/2 cups sugar

1. Place the raspberries in a food processor fitted with a steel blade and puree. Press through a strainer to remove seeds.
2. Add framboise and sugar and stir until dissolved.
3. Freeze in your ice-cream maker, following the instructions.

Yield: 2 quarts

Raspberry Liqueur

Fill a quart canning jar with freshly picked ripe raspberries for the best flavor. Add three to five black peppercorns, preferably Telicherry, 1/4 cup sugar, and fill to top with good quality vodka. Screw on a clean lid and place in a dark, cool cupboard for one month. Remove and strain liquid. The berries will be white because their color and essence will have drained into the vodka. Fill a clean glass bottle with the liquid, cap tightly with a cork or other cap, and store in a cool cupboard for one month more.
The liqueur, now ready to drink, will have a strong raspberry flavor.
In following years, you can adjust the amount of sugar to your particular taste.

Yield: 1 1/2 pints

Blueberries (*Vaccinium* species)

You will see different members of this species growing throughout the United States in acidic soil in locations ranging from swamps to mountains: some are small, low-growing shrubs, while others can reach a height of fifteen feet. Blueberries are usually found in spots where they can get a good amount of sunshine, such as open areas along the sides of roads or at the edge of woods. The fruit is light blue to blue-black in color, covered with a grayish powder, and has numerous, soft seeds. When picking, look at the top of the berries for the five-parted crown that tells you they are edible (not necessarily choice). Poisonous blue-colored berries do not have crowns. A host of wildlife lives on blueberry fruit and foliage, and many historical journals have recorded the Native Americans' extensive use of blueberries and the similar huckleberry. A traditional harvesting practice is to spread a sheet or blanket under a bush and shake the bush, causing the ripe berries to fall — much faster than picking berry by berry! There are two ways to keep blueberries for the winter: one is to dry them in the sun like the Native Americans did (or in an electric dehydrator); the other is to freeze them quickly on a tray, then pack them in plastic bags for storage.

We like the following blueberry cake warm with whipped cream for dessert or at room temperature with morning coffee.

Sabra's Blueberry Cake

3 cups blueberries
2 teaspoons cinnamon
2 cups plus 2 additional tablespoons sugar
3 cups all-purpose flour
3 teaspoons baking powder
1 teaspoon salt
1 cup canola oil
4 large eggs
1/4 cup lemon juice
1 tablespoon vanilla
Whipped cream or ice cream

1. *Preheat oven to 375°F.*
2. *Lightly oil or spray a nine-inch tube pan and set aside.*
3. *Combine blueberries, cinnamon, and two tablespoons of sugar and set aside.*
4. *Sift the flour into a large bowl, add two cups sugar, baking powder, and salt, and stir. Make a well in the center, pour in the canola oil, eggs, lemon juice, and vanilla.*
5. *Beat with a wooden spoon until well blended, and gently fold in blueberries. Spoon the batter into the pan and smooth the top.*
6. *Bake one hour or until the sides begin to pull away from the pan, the surface is golden, and a tester inserted in the center comes out clean. Check at forty-five minutes and lightly cover with foil if the top is getting too brown.*
7. *Remove pan from the oven and let stand until warm before transferring cake to a plate. Serve immediately with whipped cream or ice cream.*

Serves 8-10

One of the freshest and simplest desserts is a wild-fruit summer pudding, of which there are several versions. I make one from crustless bread fashioned into the bottom and sides of a pudding basin, then filled with gently cooked fresh blueberries, raspberries, blackberries — whatever — with lots of sugar. After sealing the top with more bread, I let it sit for a day so that the juice and fruit flavors soak throughout. Turn it out of the pudding basin and serve with concentrated extra juice, and top with fresh cream.

Plums (*Prunus* species)

The two types of plums you are most likely to encounter are the wild plum (*Prunus americana*), a small tree that grows in moist soil in the eastern half of the United States, and the beach plum (*Prunus maritima*), a low shrub that grows in sandy coastal soil from Maine to Delaware, where my wife remembers picking them as a child. The wild plum bears small, red or yellow fruit from late August through September, and the beach plum has sweet, juicy, purple fruit. Plums dry and freeze well and are favorites for jams, jellies, and pies.

Beach Plum Clafouti

1 1/2 pounds beach plums
2 tablespoons sugar
1 tablespoon flour (optional)
1/2 cup all-purpose flour
1/4 cup sugar
1/4 teaspoon salt
3 tablespoons sour cream
2 eggs
1/2 teaspoon vanilla extract
3/4 cup whole milk
2 teaspoons butter
Confectioner's sugar

1. Preheat oven to 375°F.
2. Cut plums in half and remove stones. Coat the plums in the two tablespoons of sugar and also the one tablespoon of flour, if very juicy. Set aside.
3. In a large mixing bowl, combine flour, sugar, salt, sour cream, and eggs, and mix lightly. Add vanilla and milk and beat until blended.
4. Place butter in a pie plate and set in the oven for one minute to melt. Remove from oven and swirl butter to cover bottom. Pour in enough batter to coat the bottom and bake one or two minutes until firm.
5. Remove from oven and arrange the plums evenly over the cooked batter. Pour remaining batter on top. Bake about thirty minutes until puffed up and firm.
Serve immediately, or later at room temperature, dusted with sifted confectioner's sugar.

Yield: 6 servings

Currants (*Ribes* species)

Currant berries — red, yellow, or black — are found in drooping clusters on shrubs of different shapes ranging from one to six feet tall. The many species — some escapees to the wild from cultivation — generally prefer cool, moist soil, and tend to grow in woods, ravines, and along streams. It may be hard to find abundant wild currant bushes because there was a large eradication program around the turn of the century when it was discovered that a fungus killing white pines needed currants to survive. If you do find them, the fresh berries, although tart, provide a wonderful, rich flavor for desserts, jams, and wines.

Wild Grapes (*Vitis* species)

The dozens of native grapes growing all across the country in temperate climates were an important food source for Native Americans as well as settlers. Vigorous trailing or tendril-climbing vines grow towards the light on the edges of woods, along stream banks, and on trees or fences. The grapes receiving the most sun generally taste best. The broad leaves are heart-shaped with saw-toothed edges, and the greenish flowers give way to fruits from amber to blue to dark purple in color and that ripen in late summer or early fall. Many species are a bit too acid to enjoy fresh, but will still turn into excellent juices, jams, pies, or wine. The leaves also are edible and can be blanched and used to wrap around meat or rice mixtures as is done in Middle Eastern cooking. Note: Use your guidebook and do not confuse grapes with Canada moonseed, which has bitter, poisonous fruit.

The finished drink after maturing, served with homemade elder flower sorbet

Common Elder (*Sambucus canadensis*)

The fragrant, white flowers of this shrub grow in flat, umbrella-like clusters. Appearing from mid-June to July, they serve as a source of champagne and wine and are often eaten in pancakes and fritters. The shrub grows in moist soil, often in thickets, and produces tiny purplish-black berries, also in clusters, which make wonderful jam. It is recommended that berries not be eaten raw.

In the past, elder flowers or bruised elder leaves were hung indoors to keep away flies. John Evelyn, in 1664, recommended that the blossoms be infused in vinegar as a salad ingredient. In Victorian times, households kept bottles of elder flower water for sunburn and to remove freckles. An infusion or tea of elder flowers has been used for skin problems and internally for colds, flu, gas, and upset stomachs.

Tommy's Elder Flower Cordial

20 elder flower heads
2 lemons, sliced
1 orange, sliced
2 pounds sugar
1 ounce white vinegar
2 pints boiling water

1. *Place all ingredients in nonreactive saucepan, and pour in boiling water.*
2. *Bring to a boil, dissolving sugar. Remove from heat, stir, and cover.*
3. *Let sit for four days, stirring once each day.*
4. *Strain through cheesecloth, funnel into glass bottles with screw tops.*
5. *Keep in the refrigerator or in a cool, dark place.*
6. *Serve one part cordial to five parts water (or to taste) over ice, with a sprig of mint.*

Yield: 2 pints

Staghorn Sumac (*Rhus typhina*)

No doubt you have often seen thickets of sumac, distinctive in winter with their rusty fruit clusters still hanging on. You may not have realized that this same fruit makes a lovely cold summer drink. The time to pick the fruit clusters is in late summer when the berries are bright red and covered with hairs, before rains have a chance to wash away their acid. Touch the ripe fruit with your finger, then press your finger to your tongue and you will detect the sharp taste of ascorbic acid — vitamin C.

One summer we made sumac "lemonade" by placing several clusters in a stainless steel bowl, crushing them gently with a potato masher, and covering them with cold water. After they sat for about twenty minutes, we removed the clusters and strained the resulting pink liquid. You have to make this to your own taste: if it seems too weak, soak more clusters in the same water and strain; if too strong, add water.
Sweeten and chill before serving.

Other edible red-fruited sumacs include dwarf sumac (*R. copallina*) and smooth sumac (*R. glabra*). Note: Do not confuse these sumacs with poison sumac, which has clusters of small, white berries.

Conclusion

E.M. Forster's novel *Howards End* has passages evoking the pleasure of retreating to a charming old house in the bluebell forest.
When the royalties from his books began to pile up, Forster acquired such a place, complete with its own woods. Then the gentle, ecologically minded democrat became a narrow-minded conservative when he said, "It was intersected, blast it, by a public footpath." He wanted solitude and the exclusive freedom of the surroundings. Strangers, whether humans, deer, or squirrels, would be after *his* flowers, fruits, and nuts. He didn't much like the idea, either, that his favorite birds might fly off to a more attractive or rewarding location.

Having a place in the country, it is sometimes difficult to overcome the territorial imperative buried in all of us. It has taken me some years to stop worrying about hunters' guns, or chain saw, snowmobile, and heavy equipment noises sounding nearer than they should.
Rarely is there something amiss; we all do get along; and I personally feel encouraged that the countryside where I live is returning in large part to its natural state more quickly than we can destroy it.
I keep discovering some new plant, or new use of a familiar one, and changes in natural conditions and habitats that further encourage my confidence and sense of security in living within the countryside.
And perhaps even leaving it more naturally productive for all species doesn't seem now to be as difficult as I thought it would be when we first arrived and began to make a home.

Bibliography

Abbey, Edward. *Desert Solitaire.* New York: Ballantine Books, 1971.

Angier, Bradford. *Field Guide to Edible Wild Plants.* Harrisburg, Pennsylvania: Stackpole Books, 1974.

Baron, Robert C., ed., *The Garden and Farm Books of Thomas Jefferson.* Golden, Colorado: Fulcrum, Inc., 1987.

Buchanan, Rita. *A Dyer's Garden.* Loveland, Colorado: Interweave Press, 1995.

Coon, Nelson. *Using Wayside Plants.* New York: Hearthside Press, 1969.

Crowhurst, Adrienne. *The Weed Cookbook.* New York: Lancer Books, Inc., 1972.

Erichsen-Brown, Charlotte. *Medicinal and Other Uses of North American Plants.* New York: Dover Publications, 1989.

Emery, Carla: *The Encyclopedia of Country Living.* Seattle: Sasquatch Books, 1994.

Foster, Steven, and James A. Duke. *A Field Guide to Medicinal Plants.* Boston: Houghton Mifflin Company, 1990.

Gibbons, Euell. *Stalking the Wild Asparagus.* New York: David McKay Company, 1962.

Heat-Moon, William Least. *PrairyErth.* Boston: Houghton Mifflin, 1991.

Hillaby, John. *Journey through Love.* London: Constable and Company, 1976.

Lincoff, Gary H. *The Audubon Society Field Guide to North American Mushrooms.* New York: Knopf, 1981.

Little, Elbert L. *The Audubon Society Field Guide to North American Trees, Western Region.* New York: Knopf, 1980.

_____. *The Audubon Society Field Guide to North American Trees, Eastern Region.* New York: Knopf, 1980.

Niering, William A., and Nancy C. Olmstead. *National Audubon Society Field Guide to North American Wildflowers, Eastern Region.* New York: Knopf, 1979.

Olsen, Larry Dean. *Outdoor Survival Skills.* Chicago, Chicago Review Press, 1997.

Organic Gardening Magazine. *The Encyclopedia of Organic Gardening.* Emmaus, Pennsylvania: Rodale Press, 1978.

Peterson, Lee. *A Field Guide to Edible Wild Plants of Eastern and Central North America.* Boston: Houghton Mifflin Company, 1978.

Phillips, Roger. *Mushrooms of North America.* Boston: Little, Brown and Company, 1991.

_____. *Wild Food.* Boston: Little, Brown and Company, 1983.

Phillips, Roger, and Nicky Foy. *Herbs.* London: Pan Books Ltd., 1990.

Reader's Digest. *Back to Basics.* Pleasantville, New York: The Reader's Digest Association, Inc., 1981.

_____. *North American Wildlife.* Pleasantville, New York: The Reader's Digest Association, Inc., 1982.

Stary, Frantisek. *The Natural Guide to Medicinal Herbs and Plants.* London: Treasure Press, 1991.

Whitaker, John O., Jr. *The Audubon Society Field Guide to North American Mammals.* New York: Knopf, 1980.

Acknowledgments:

I would like to thank the following for their help in the preparation of this book:

Bill Byrne; Tommy Candler and Alan Plaistowe; Canterbury Shaker Village;
Russell A. Cohen; Ronnie and Becky Dodd; Dorothy Elliott; Liza Fosburgh; Michael and Neyla Freeman;
A. Blake Gardner; John and Betty Holmes; Marc and Vivienne Jaffe; Arthur Magri; Hal Malde;
Terry McAweeney; Roger Phillips and Nicky Foy; Paul and Elaine Rocheleau; Brian and Lizzie Sanders;
Judith Storie.

Photo Credits:

Bill Byrne, 23, 27, 38, 40 *bottom,* 41 *bottom,* 44 *top and bottom,* 45, 46, 47, 48 *right,* 49 *top, bottom, and right,* 50, 53 *top,* 107, 108 *right.*

Tommy Candler, 69 *right,* 70, 121, 122, 123, 145, 149 *bottom right,* 151, 152 top, 156 *left.*

Michael Freeman, 48 *left,* 71 *top,* 83.

A. Blake Gardner, 7 *top,* 9, 14, 15, 16 *top,* 26, 29, 30, 31, 32, 33, 35, 36-37, 39, 40 *top,* 41 *top,* 42, 43, 51, 52, 54, 56-57, 59, 61, 62, 63, 64, 65, 66, 67, 75, 76-77, 78, 79, 80, 81, 84, 85, 86, 87, 88-89, 94-95, 98, 104, 120, 130, 155 *left and right.*

David Larkin, 7 *bottom,* 11, 16 *bottom,* 17, 18, 19, 34, 53 *bottom,* 55, 58, 71 *bottom,* 72 *left and right,* 73, 74, 96 *bottom,* 97 *bottom,* 99, 100, 101, 102, 103, 106, 111, 112, 113, 134, 135, 136, 137 *top,* 146 *top,* 147 *left,* 148 *bottom,* 157 *right.*

Roger Phillips, 2, 3, 20, 21, 22, 58 *left and right,* 91, 92, 93, 96 *top,* 97 *top,* 105, 108 *left,* 109, 110, 114, 115, 116, 117, 118, 119, 121, 124, 125, 126, 127, 128, 129, 131, 133, 137 *bottom,* 138, 139, 140, 141, 142, 143, 144, 146 *bottom,* 147 *left,* 148-149 *top,* 149 *bottom left,* 150, 152 *bottom,* 153, 154, 156 *right,* 157 *left.*

Paul Rocheleau, 8 *bottom,* 10, 12, 28, 72 *top,* 158.